Study Guide

for

Senna and Siegel's

Introduction to Criminal Justice

Eighth Edition

Roy J. Royberg
San Jose State University

West / Wadsworth
I⊤P® An International Thomson Publishing Company

Belmont, CA • Albany, NY • Boston • Cincinnati • Johannesburg • London • Madrid • Melbourne
Mexico City • New York • Pacific Grove, CA • Scottsdale, AZ • Singapore • Tokyo • Toronto

For more information, contact Wadsworth Publishing Company, 10 Davis Drive, Belmont, CA 94002, or electronically at http://www.wadsworth.com

International Thomson Publishing Europe
Berkshire House
168-173 High Holborn
London, WC1V 7AA, United Kingdom

Nelson ITP, Australia
102 Dodds Street
South Melbourne
Victoria 3205 Australia

Nelson Canada
1120 Birchmount Road
Scarborough, Ontario
Canada M1K 5G4

International Thomson Publishing Southern Africa
Building 18, Constantia Square
138 Sixteenth Road, P.O. Box 2459
Halfway House, 1685 South Africa

International Thomson Editores
Seneca, 53
Colonia Polanco
11560 México D.F. México

International Thomson Publishing Asia
60 Albert Street
#15-01 Albert Complex
Singapore 189969

International Thomson Publishing Japan
Hirakawa-cho Kyowa Building, 3F
2-2-1 Hirakawa-cho, Chiyoda-ku
Tokyo 102, Japan

ISBN 0-534-54731-1

Contents

Student Introduction

This study guide has been designed and written to introduce students to the field of criminal justice by helping them master the important concepts and principles presented in *Introduction to Criminal Justice*, and to further stimulate interest in defining the problems and solutions which confront the administration of justice system. Following is a brief description of how this workbook can best be utilized in assimilating the materials in the text and in preparing you for examination.

For good use of the study guide, the following steps are suggested. First, read the **LEARNING OBJECTIVES** to familiarize yourself with the key issues that will be addressed in the chapter. Second, read the **CHAPTER SUMMARY** to get an overview of the chapter's contents. Third, review the **KEY TERMS AND CONCEPTS** to assist you in recognizing important points as they appear in the chapter. Fourth, carefully read the chapter itself. Fifth, attempt to complete the **FILL-IN REVIEWS** without the use of the text for reference.

After the FILL-IN REVIEW section has been completed, you can evaluate your accuracy by turning to the **ANSWER SECTION** at the back of the chapter. If you have problems completing some of the fill-in questions, the text should be reviewed until all the answers can be provided. To assist you in locating the correct responses, this section has been prepared in sequential order with the material in the text.

After you have studied the chapter material, you should take the **SELF TEST** as though you were actually taking an exam. This section contains True/False, Multiple Choice, Matching, and Essay questions; although most exams in introductory courses tend to be primarily multiple choice in nature, the other types of questions in this section will help you to assess your knowledge of the materials. If you do not do as well on the SELF TEST as anticipated, you may wish to intensify your study of the textbook and further your review of the study guide.

We hope you enjoy you study of crime and justice in the United States. A special thanks and my gratitude are extended to John Ryan Wilson and Shannon Neal Thomas for their contributions to the preparation of this study guide.

1   Crime and Criminal Justice

LEARNING OBJECTIVES

1. Explain several aspects of the crime problem.

2. Define the concept and the study of criminal justice.

3. Describe the role of the three branches of government in the criminal justice system.

4. Explain how discretion can be exercised by police officers.

5. Distinguish between the functions of the lower criminal, superior, and appellate courts.

6. Identify and discuss several problems facing the corrections system today.

7. Discuss the stages of the criminal justice process, from initial contact to post-release.

8. Discuss the informal justice system and the role it plays.

CHAPTER SUMMARY

The term criminal justice refers to an area of knowledge devoted to controlling crime through the operation and administration of police, court, and correctional agencies. Criminal justice is an interdisciplinary field of study that uses knowledge from many disciplines in an attempt to understand what causes people to commit crimes and how to deal with the crime problem. In sum, criminal justice consists of the study of crime and of the agencies concerned with its prevention and control.

Criminal justice is both a system and a process. It is a **system** in that it functions cooperatively among several primary agencies: police, courts, and corrections. The **process** of criminal justice consists of steps the offender follows from the initial investigation through trial, sentencing, and appeal. The modern era of criminal justice study was ushered in during the late 1960's with the **Crime Commission** study of America's crime problem and the passage of the **Safe Streets and Crime Control Act** which funded the Law Enforcement Assistance Administration (LEAA).

Chapter 1

Each branch of government is involved in the criminal justice system. The legislature defines what is prohibited by law and prescribes penalties as well as providing financial support for criminal justice programs. The judiciary is responsible for judicial review, ensuring that the law meets constitutional standards. The executive branch has the power of appointment of figures such as judges and heads of administrative agencies such as police chiefs. Executives also play a major leadership role in criminal justice matters and maintain both the power to develop programs and veto legislation.

The three basic components of the criminal justice system include the police, the courts, and correction agencies. The **police** are involved in law enforcement, the **courts** deal with the administration of justice, and **correction** agencies deal with probation, incarceration and parole.

Often, the criminal justice system works informally to quickly settle cases. The courtroom work group, consisting of the prosecutor, defense attorney, judge and other courtroom personnel helps to streamline the process with plea bargaining and other alternatives. Most criminal acts that are deemed serious receive the entire complement of the criminal justice process, from arrest to trial. However, cases that are less serious may be settled quickly when a bargain between the prosecution and the defense can be reached such as a guilty plea in return for a more lenient sentence, dropping of charges or other considerations.

This informal justice process has been compared by Samuel Walker to a four-layer cake, known as the **"Wedding Cake"** Model of Justice. Cases in the first layer of the cake are usually celebrated cases receiving the full array of criminal justice procedures. In the second layer are the serious felonies: rapes, robberies and burglaries. Level three of the wedding cake consists of either less serious offenses, committed by young or first-time offenders, and/or involving people who knew each other or were otherwise related. Level three crimes typically results in a probationary sentence or intermediate sanction. The fourth layer of the cake is made up of the many types of misdemeanors, handled by lower criminal courts in assembly-line fashion. Few defendants insist on exercising their constitutional rights because the delay would cost them valuable time and money.

Finally, career alternatives in criminal justice include those in the social service sector, law enforcement, law and courts, and teaching and research.

KEY TERMS AND CONCEPTS

Criminal Justice System
Predatory Criminals
Nonintervention
Sentencing
Stigma
Complaint
DARE
Discretion
Deinstitutionalization
Law Enforcement Assistance
Administration (LEAA)
Adversary System
Probation
Rehabilitation
Restorative justice
Judicial review

Intermediate Sanctions
Probable Cause
In-Presence Requirement
Bill of Indictment
Information
Arraignment
Appeal
Nolle Prosequi
Courtroom Work Group
Indigent Defendants
Recidivism
Due Process
Bail
Legalization
"Social engineering"

FILL-IN REVIEW

1. The debate over the proper course for crime control can be originally traced to Cesare Beccaria's 1764 publication *"On _____ and _____."*

2. The first police agency was the _____ Metropolitan Police.

3. The _____ _____ Commission, created in 1919, acted as a citizens advocate group and kept track of the ongoing activities of local justice agencies.

4. The _____ Commission, created in 1931, helped usher in the era of treatment and rehabilitation.

5. The _____ _____ Assistance Administration provided federal funding to local and state justice agencies.

6. The three components of the criminal justice system in the United States are the _____ , the _____ , and _____ .

7. Police departments are those public agencies created to maintain _____ , enforce the _____ law, provide emergency services, keep traffic on streets and highways moving freely, and create a sense of _____ safety.

3

8.   The superior courts, or major trial courts, have general jurisdiction over all _____ offenses but ordinarily concentrate on _____ cases.

9.   The highest state court is a _____, or _____ court, whose functions are similar to those of the United States Supreme Court in the federal judicial system.

10.   The _____ is a public official who represents the government and presents its case against the defendant, who is charged with a violation of the criminal law.

11.   State courts must provide _____ defendants charged with criminal offenses legal representation where the possibility of _____ exists.

12.   The system of corrections has many responsibilities, including protecting _____, deterring crime, and _____ offenders.

13.   _____ is a judicial action or legal disposition that allows the offender to remain in the community subject to conditions imposed by court order, under the supervision of a _____ officer.

14.   The jail holds offenders convicted of minor crimes or _____, and _____ people awaiting trial or involved in other proceedings.

15.   The jail is ordinarily operated by _____ government and is often under the jurisdiction of the _____ Sheriff.

16.   The _____ _____ considers cases in a closed hearing in which only the _____ presents evidence.

17.   _____ is a money bond to insure the return of a criminal defendant.

18.   An _____ occurs when the police take a person in custody and the suspect believes that he or she has lost his or her _____.

19.   The _____, prosecutor, defense attorney, and other court personnel form the _____ work group, which encourages plea bargaining and other alternatives leading to quick resolution.

20.   The informal justice process has been described by Samuel Walker as a four layer _____ _____ model of justice.

21.   The modern criminal justice system consists of over _____ public agencies.

22.   _____workers supervise offenders after their release from correctional treatment.

23.   The criminal justice system has been referred to as an _____conveyer belt.

SELF TEST

True/False

24.   Crime rates have been rising during the first half of the 1990's.

25.   Most people view crime as a major social problem.

26.   The criminal justice is a very loosely organized collection of agencies.

27.   Criminal justice is an agency of social control designed to deal with legal misbehavior.

28.   Academic institutions have **not** been a resource for those trying to find solutions to the crime problem.

29.   The various elements of the criminal justice system - such as police, courts, and corrections - can be described as well coordinated and operating in unison.

30.   A police officer is not allowed to use discretion while on the job.

31.   "Back room justice" refers to a system that has developed which encourages defendants to plead guilty in exchange for special consideration such as reducing the charges.

32.   The criminal court judge is responsible for sentencing the offender.

33.   The superior courts, or major trial courts, deal with the largest number of criminal offenses.

34.   State supreme courts are appellate courts that conduct criminal trials and decide questions of fact.

35.   Appellate courts deal with procedural errors arising in the lower courts that are considered a violation of rights guaranteed by state and/or the United States Constitution.

36.   Where a trial is required in the lower courts, it often occurs before a judge rather than before a jury.

37.   The prosecutor and defense attorney are opponents in the adversary system.

38. The Eighth Amendment of the United States Constitution gives the accused the right to have the assistance of defense counsel.

39. Prisons or penitentiaries are state-operated facilities that house misdemeanor offenders sentenced by the criminal courts.

40. Typically, inmates serve three-fourths of their sentence.

41. To make an arrest in a misdemeanor, the officer must have witnessed the crime personally.

42. Bail is used to pay for the court costs.

43. Approximately ninety percent of all cases end in a plea bargain, rather than a criminal trial.

44. Incarceration is a form of disposition.

45. Intermediate sanctions are both more costly and intrusive than traditional methods of incarceration.

46. A defendant has the right to appeal his conviction in an appellate court.

47. Most arrests result in conviction.

MULTIPLE CHOICE

48. The debate over proper crime control can be traced to the 1776 publication by:

    a. Cesare Beccaria
    b. Rene Decarte
    c. John Douglas
    d. Miguel De Cervantes

49. In 1931, president Herbert Hoover appointed the _____ commission to make a detailed analysis of the U.S. justice system.

    a. Wickersham
    b. Hoover
    c. Walker
    d. Ford

50. Which of the following would a Supreme Court be likely to perform:

    a. affirm lower court decisions
    b. review questions of fact from the original trial
    c. conduct a criminal trial
    d. both a and b

51. When an offender is sentenced by the court to a period of confinement, responsibility for custody and rehabilitation lies with the:

    a. court
    b. correction agency
    c. district attorney
    d. none of the above

52. A prosecutor may be called a(n):

    a. attorney general
    b. defense lawyer
    c. judge
    d. none of the above

53. The criminal justice system is a political entity whose basic framework is lodged within what system of government?

    a. Legislative
    b. Judicial
    c. Executive
    d. all of the above

54. The primary responsibility of legislatures in the justice system is to:

    a. define criminal behavior
    b. establish criminal penalties
    c. both a and b
    d. none of the above

55. _____ have the rights to overturn laws which are in conflict with the constitution.

    a. courts
    b. legislators
    c. executives
    d. none of the above

56. Which of the following would be unlikely to happen at an arraignment.

    a. defendant would be informed of his/her constitutional rights
    b. prosecutors would demonstrate that a trial was warranted
    c. formal charges would be read to the defendant
    d. both a and c

57. Which extralegal factor(s) may influence the decision outcome in the criminal justice process.

    a. available evidence
    b. suspect's race or class
    c. suspect's prior record
    d. seriousness of charges

58. If a felony case is turned over to the district attorney's office, the prosecutor can then.

    a. bring the case before a grand jury
    b. bring the case to a preliminary hearing
    c. *nolle prosequi* the case
    d. all of the above

59. The research arm of the United States Justice Department is the:

    a. National Institute of Justice
    b. Battelle Institute
    c. National Council on Criminal Delinquency
    d. Law Enforcement Assistance Administration

60. What percentage of arrestees test positive for at least one drug.

    a. 40%
    b. 50%
    c. 60%
    d. 70%

61. Approximately _____ arrests occur annually.

    a. 6 million
    b. 10 million
    c. 14 million
    d. 28 million

MATCHING

62.	Academic institutions	A.	Exercise discretion
63.	*Nolle prosequi*	B.	Decision by prosecutor
64.	Police officers	C.	Asset for crime solution
65.	Arraignment	D.	State proves probable cause
66.	Grand Jury	E.	Criminal trial held
67.	Postconviction remedies	F.	Opportunity to appeal
68.	Adjudication	G.	Money bond
69.	Bail	H.	Formal charges read

ESSAY QUESTIONS

70. Briefly discuss the historical development of the criminal justice system.

71. List and briefly discuss the functions of the major component parts of the criminal justice system.

72. Describe Walker's "wedding cake" model, and give an example of a crime at each of the four levels and the expected disposition.

73. Describe the differences between the formal and informal justice systems. Is it fair to treat some offenders informally and not others?

74. Define the roles of the prosecutor and the defense attorney.

CHAPTER ONE ANSWER SECTION

FILL-IN REVIEW

1. *Crime, Punishment*
2. London
3. Chicago Crime
4. Wickersham
5. Law Enforcement
6. courts, corrections
7. order, criminal, community
8. criminal, felony
9. Supreme, Appellate
10. prosecutor
11. indigent, incarceration
12. society, rehabilitating
13. Probation, probation
14. misdemeanors, detains
15. local, county
16. grand jury, prosecutor
17. Bail
18. arrest, liberty
19. judge, work group
20. "wedding cake"
21. 55,000
22. Social
23. assembly line

SELF TEST

True/False

24.	F	36.	T
25.	T	37.	T
26.	T	38.	F
27.	T	39.	F
28.	F	40.	F
29.	F	41.	T
30.	F	42.	F
31.	T	43.	T
32.	T	44.	T
33.	T	45.	F
34.	F	46.	T
35.	T	47.	F

MULTIPLE CHOICE

48.	D	55.	A
49.	D	56.	D
50.	D	57.	B
51.	B	58.	D
52.	A	59.	A
53.	D	60.	C
54.	C	61.	C

MATCHING

62.	C
63.	B
64.	A
65.	H
66.	D
67.	F
68.	E
69.	G

2   The Nature of Crime and Victimization

LEARNING OBJECTIVES

1.   Explain the concept of crime.

2.   Discuss how survey data and record data are used.

3.   Describe the Uniform Crime Reports and how crime is measured by them; discuss several major methodological problems regarding validity.

4.   Discuss the differences in crime trends in other countries and what accounts for them.

5.   List and discuss at least four important issues regarding patterns of crime in America.

6.   Discuss the advantages of self-report studies.

7.   Describe the National Crime Victimization Survey and how crime is measured by the survey; discuss several methodological problems regarding the validity of the NCVS.

8.   Explain the general pattern of victimization including victim characteristics, ecology and relationship to criminal.

9.   Discuss what might account for the apparent rise in female criminal activities.

10.   Explain the crime trends since 1980 and the possible explanations for such trends.

CHAPTER SUMMARY

Crimes are behaviors that are harmful to a majority of citizens and therefore prohibited or controlled by criminal law. Criminal justice seeks to understand the nature and cause of crime and victimization in order to create effective reduction programs.

Criminal justice data comes from a variety of sources. **Survey data** is comprised of information obtained from interviews and questionnaires focusing on people's behaviors, attitudes and beliefs. This data proves an invaluable source of information on the nature and extent of criminal victimization and particular crime problems, such as drug use, which are rarely reported. One important survey of this type is the annual high school drug survey conducted by researchers at the University of Michigan's Institute for Social Research. **Record data** comes from a variety of sources, including police departments, courts, social service centers and schools, also provide a significant amount of criminal justice data. It includes: cohort studies, measuring a group with shared characteristics over an extended period of time; observational data; and life histories.

The **Uniform Crime Reports** (UCRs), prepared by the Federal Bureau of Investigation, are the best known and cited source of criminal statistics. The FBI receives and compiles reports from over 16,000 police departments serving a majority of the population; consequently, the UCRs are based on crimes reported to the police. **Index crimes**, also know as **Part I** offenses, are the major unit of analysis of the UCRs and include: murder and nonnegligent manslaughter, forcible rape, robbery, aggravated assault, burglary, larceny, arson, and auto theft. **Part II** offenses, which include all other crimes (excluding traffic violations), except those classified as Part I, are also recorded in the UCRs.

It has been estimated that fewer than half of all crimes are actually reported to the police. This suggests that UCR data does not give a realistic or complete story of crime. In the late 1960's a number of pioneering studies found that victims could tell us a lot about the crime problem. This early research encouraged development of the most widely used and most extensive survey to date, the **National Crime Victimization Survey** (NCVS). The NCVS is conducted by the Bureau of Justice Statistics of the U.S. Department of Justice in cooperation with the U.S. Bureau of the Census. The annual surveys ask about victimizations suffered during the six months preceding the interview including personal and household larcenies, burglary, motor vehicle theft, assaults, robberies, and rape.

While many crime victims do not report criminal incidents to the police, evidence indicates that the crimes reported tend to be less serious. Consequently, UCR and NCVS data may be more similar than some critics believe. These data indicate some distinct patterns of crime: it occurs more often in large cities, during the summer, at night; the far west and southern states experience more crime than do midwestern or New England states; males, minorities, the poor, and the young victimize people who share their personal characteristics.

Another method of collecting data is through the use of **self-report surveys**. Self-report surveys ask respondents to tell about their criminal and deviant activities. One main advantage of using this method is that it measures the so-called "dark figures" of crime--such as drug use, gambling, and alcohol abuse, which often remain unreported in official data sources and victimization surveys. Another advantage of this method is that it can be used to collect personal information from offenders such as IQ, attitudes, values, and family relationships, which are unavailable from other crime data sources.

Many recent studies have begun to focus attention on victimization and the role of the victim in crime. The cause of victimization has been linked to life-style and activity.

KEY TERMS AND CONCEPTS

Crime
Criminal Law
Social Control
Moral Entrepreneurs
Conflict View
Probability Samples
Part I Offenses
Part II Offenses
Uniform Crime Reports (UCRs)
Chronic Offenders
Interactionist View

Instrumental Crimes
Expressive Crimes
Participant Observation
Life History
Index Crimes
Relative Deprivation
Self-Report Surveys
National Crime Victimization Surveys (NCVS)
Desistance
Aging Out
Cohort Research

FILL-IN REVIEW

1. _____ are behaviors that are harmful to a majority of citizens and have been controlled or prohibited by _____ law.

2. _____ _____ are those who attempt to use their economic, social, and political influence to impose their moral standards on the rest of society.

3. Survey data is comprised of information obtained from _____ and _____ focusing on people's behaviors, attitudes, beliefs, and abilities.

4. The Uniform _____ _____ _____ are best known and most widely cited source of criminal statistics.

The Nature of Crime and Victimization

5. The police _____ or solved approximately 20 percent of all crimes _____ to them.

6. Index crimes include _____ and nonnegligent manslaughter, forcible _____, _____ aggravated _____, _____, larceny, _____, and _____ theft.

7. Areas with rural and suburban populations are more likely to have much _____ crime rates than large _____ areas.

8. UCR data consistently shows that males have a _____ crime rate than females. However, in the last _____ the female crime rate has _____ at a faster rate than males.

9. Almost _____ percent of all arrests involve people between the ages of _____ and _____ .

10. Two major problems with the UCRs are citizen neglect to _____ criminal acts to police and variations in law _____ practices.

11. _____ surveys are particularly effective in monitoring adolescent _____ use.

12. The most widely used and most extensive victim survey to date is the _____ _____ _____ Survey.

13. NCVS data indicate that members of the lowest income categories were by far the most likely to be victims of _____ crimes and most personal _____ crimes.

14. _____ _____ refers to extensive, in depth interviews with individuals who have had experience in crime.

15. Although participant observational data may involve _____ risks, it can also provide invaluable _____ into crime and criminal offenders.

16. The three main measures of crime are _____ data, _____ data and _____ data.

17. Theft victimization is more likely to occur to those in the _____ income classification.

18.   Age is _____ proportional to criminality.

19.   _____crimes, such as rape and assault, express rage, frustration and anger against society while _____ crimes result from the desire to obtain goods and services unattainable by conventional means.

SELF TEST

True/False

20.   A probability sample is used in surveys because of the strong likelihood it represents the general population.

21.   Property crime rates have remained relatively stable during the past decade, while murder rates have significantly increased.

22.   The United States leads the world in murder, rape and robbery rates.

23.   In the past decade, violence has dramatically increased in the U.S.

24.   Police solve three times more violent crimes than property crimes.

25.   Crime rates for teens should continue to decrease over the next decade.

26.   African-Americans are arrested for murder, rape and robbery at a rate lower than their relative representation in the population.

27.   The peak age for property crime is sixteen, and for violence, it is eighteen.

28.   American citizens are believed to report seventy-five percent of all criminal and delinquent acts to the police.

29.   Self-report studies measure the so-called "dark figures" of crime.

30.   Self-report studies indicate that criminals and delinquents specialize in one type of crime over another.

31.   Self-report studies indicate youth crime is concentrated among middle-class kids.

32.   The Institute for Social Research (ISR) data indicates that since 1980, American students have significantly increased the extent and frequency of their drug abuse.

33. Men are about twice as likely as women to be victims of robbery and assault.

34. African-Americans are more likely than either whites or hispanics to become victims of crime.

35. Like the UCRs, the NCVS and victimization surveys, suffer from some methodological problems.

36. Changes in the overall crime rate may reflect the way citizens report crime to the police and the way police departments record the results, rather than any actual charge in the amount or rate of crime.

37. Index crimes are also known as Part I offenses and are reported to the FBI on a monthly basis by law enforcement agencies.

38. The probability of the average twelve year old becoming the victim of a violent crime sometime during their lifespan is over 80 percent.

39. Unreported crimes tend to be more serious offenses.

40. Punishment-oriented strategies have proved effective in controlling crime.

41. Most criminal acts are intraracial in nature.

MULTIPLE CHOICE

42. Which of the following are type II offenses.

   a. drug offenses
   b. traffic violations
   c. murder
   d. b and c

43. Which of the following is **not** considered an Index Crime of the Uniform Crime Reports:

   a. nonnegligent manslaughter
   b. assault and battery
   c. robbery
   d. murder

44.   The United States robbery rate (1990) is approximately _____ times greater than that of Japan.

   a.   10
   b.   50
   c.   150
   d.   500

45.   The FBI estimates that approximately _____ percent of all index crimes are cleared by arrest.

   a.   5
   b.   10
   c.   20
   d.   30

46.   When the UCR indicates that the murder rate was 7.4 in 1996, it means that about 7 people in every _____ fell victim to crime between January 1 and December 31 of 1996.

   a.   1,000
   b.   10,000
   c.   100,000
   d.   1,000,000

47.   Major methodological problems associated with the UCR's include:

   a.   many citizens do not report crimes to the police
   b.   lack of expertise by the FBI to accurately compute crime data
   c.   variations in law enforcement reporting practices
   d.   both a and c

48.   It has been estimated that almost _____ percent of all youths commit delinquent and criminal acts.

   a.   25
   b.   50
   c.   75
   d.   90

49.   Reasons given by victims for **not** reporting crime include:

a.   believing nothing can be done
b.   believing it is a private matter
c.   not wanting to get involved
d.   all of the above

50.   The National Crime Victimization Survey is associated with the:

a.   U.S. Bureau of the Census
b.   U.S. Department of Justice
c.   Bureau of Information Services
d.   both a and b

51.   The concept of the chronic offender is most closely associated with the research efforts of:

a.   Robert Merton
b.   Marvin Wolfgang
c.   Emile Durkheim
d.   Ronald Akers

52.   The chronic offender is one who:

a.   has minor and relatively few brushes with the law
b.   is building a career in crime
c.   exhibits excessively violent and destructive behavior
d.   both b and c

53.   Elderly males (over 65) are most likely to be involved in which type of crime.

a.   drunk driving
b.   shoplifting
c.   assault
d.   rape

54.   How many murders occur on average to Americans per year.

a.   5,000
b.   10,000
c.   15,000
d.   20,000

55.   UCR revisions include which of the following:

    a.   gender neutral terms
    b.   expanded crime categories
    c.   more detailed information
    d.   all of the above

56.   Which type of crime is least likely to be reported to police.

    a.   violent crime
    b.   household theft
    c.   personal theft
    d.   both a and b

57.   While comprising approximately 12 percent of the U.S. population, African-Americans account for what percent of total arrests.

    a.   15
    b.   20
    c.   25
    d.   30

MATCHING

58.   Cohort data

59.   Official data

60.   Survey data

61.   National Crime Victimization Survey (NCVS)

62.   Self-report data

63.   Part I offense

64.   Part II offense

A.   Uniform Crime Report (UCR)

B.   Measurement of criminal activity

C.   U.S. Department of Justice/ U.S. Bureau of Census

D.   Murder

E.   Assault

F.   Institute for Social Research

G.   Measure for drug use

ESSAY QUESTIONS

65. Describe your own definition of crime. Does morality play a role in shaping your ideas or is it inappropriate? Explain why.

66. List the major methodological problems associated with the UCR and NCVS and describe what each is designed to measure.

67. Regarding patterns of crime, describe what you feel are the three most significant factors relating to crime, and why.

68. Discuss whether you believe crime rates will increase or decline in the United States over the next decade. Give several reasons for your answer.

69. Is the women's liberation movement responsible for increasing the number of female offenders? Explain why, or why not.

70. If crime is a relatively routine activity, what steps should be taken to avoid becoming a victim of crime.

CHAPTER TWO ANSWER SECTION

FILL-IN REVIEW

1. Crimes, criminal
2. Moral entrepreneurs
3. interviews, questionnaires
4. Crime Reports
5. cleared, reported
6. murder, rape, robbery, assault, burglary, arson, auto
7. lower, urban
8. higher, decade, risen
9. twenty, fifteen, nineteen
10. report, enforcement
11. Self-report, drug
12. National Crime Victimization
13. violent, theft
14. Life History
15. ethical, insight
16. official, self-report, victim
17. highest
18. inversely
19. Expressive, instrumental

SELF TEST

True/False

20.	T		31.	F
21.	F		32.	T
22.	T		33.	T
23.	F		34.	T
24.	T		35.	T
25.	F		36.	T
26.	F		37.	T
27.	T		38.	T
28.	F		39.	F
29.	T		40.	F
30.	F		41.	T

MULTIPLE CHOICE

42.	A	50.	D
43.	B	51.	B
44.	C	52.	D
45.	C	53.	A
46.	C	54.	D
47.	D	55.	D
48.	D	56.	C
49.	D	57.	D

MATCHING

58.	B
59.	A
60.	F
61.	C
62.	G
63.	D
64.	E

3   Understanding Crime and Victimization

LEARNING OBJECTIVES

1. Discuss the main principles of classical theory and Cesare Beccaria's contribution to this approach of crime causation.

2. Differentiate between the concepts of incapacitation, general deterrence, and specific deterrence.

3. Discuss several biological theories and Cesare Lombroso's contribution to this approach to crime causation. Discuss the most recent biological theory.

4. List and briefly describe the four areas of study regarding the psychological approach to crime causation.

5. Differentiate between the sociological, biological and psychological theories of crime causation.

6. Compare and contrast the social structure theory and the social process theory.

7. Describe the development of deviant values.

8. Discuss the theories of female criminality and the different views relating to the theory.

9. Define anomie and strain and describe their relationship to crime.

10. Discuss Hirschi's bond theory.

11. Differentiate among the three branches of sociobiology.

12. Discuss several theories related to victimization.

CHAPTER SUMMARY

Several theoretical perspectives have attempted to explain the cause(s) of criminal behavior in hopes of creating effective crime reduction programs.

Choice theory believes in a rational criminal who weighs the potential benefits and consequences before choosing criminal activity. In this view, crime deterrence include(s) swift, certain and severe punishments. Such theories have led to situational crime prevention programs, which attempt to increase the effort needed to commit crime, increase the risks of criminal activities, and reduce the rewards of criminal behavior.

Biological theories attempt to link criminality to biochemical factors, neurological problems and genetic influences, while **psychoanalytic theories** point to early developmental problems, personality disorders, social learning and perceptual problems, as influential in criminality.

Sociological theories equate crime with a variety of social factors. The **social structure theory** contends that the U.S. is a stratified society resulting in strain, which leads to crime. The **social process theory** points to socialization a key to understanding the onset of criminality. Branches of the social process theory include learning theory, social control theory and labeling theory. The **conflict theory** views the economic and political forces operating in society as using the criminal justice system as a vehicle to control poor numbers of society. **Integrated theories** include: multi-factor theories, latent trait theories and life course theories.

The **victim precipitation** view holds that many victims actually provoke the attacks which led to their injury or death. Victimization has also been linked to life-style and activities. Criminals and victims seem to share similar personal characteristics. The **routine activities** view holds that the incidence of criminal activity is related to the nature of everyday behavioral patterns. Cohen and Felson have identified three factors to explain **predatory crime**: the supply of motivated offenders, the supply of suitable targets, and the absence of effective guardians of protection.

KEY TERMS AND CONCEPTS

Choice Theory
Classical View
Rational Criminal
General Deterrence
Specific Deterrence
Perceptual Deterrence
Recidivision
Deviance
Defensible Space
Crime Prevention Tactics
Selective Incapacitation
Sociobiology
Biochemical Factors
Neurological Factors
Genetic Factors
Psychoanalysis
Social Learning Theory
Moral Development Theory
Psychopaths
Treatment - oriented crime prevention
Stratified Society
Disorganized Neighborhood

Relative Deprivation
Gang Culture
Social Process Theory
Cultural Transmission
Differential Association
Labeling
Conflict Theory
Integration
Latent Trait Theory
Victim Precipitation
Routine Activities
Emile Durkheim
Robert Merton
Travis Hirschi
Female Criminality
Lawrence Cohen
Marcus Felson
Chronic Recidivist
Anomie
Social Structure Theory
Culture of Poverty
Strain

FILL-IN REVIEW

1.   Experts on serial killers estimate that fewer than _____ are active at any one time.

2.   _____ theories of crime causation examine personality, development, cognition and social learning.

3.   Biological theories attempt to explain crime and aggressive behavior with biochemical, _____, and _____factors.

4.   The _____ theory holds that criminals weigh the potential _____ and _____ of their action, braking the law where there appear to be immediate benefits absent the threat of long-term risks.

Understanding Crime and Victimization

5. The classical view of crime maintains that _____ chooses between _____ and _____ activities.

6. For punishment to act as an effective deterrent, it must be _____, _____ and _____.

7. General deterrence assumes criminals to be _____.

8. _____ deterrence is the belief that actual punishment, as opposed to threat of punishment, should deter _____ offenses.

9. According to Oscar Newman's research regarding _____ space, crime can be prevented by modifying residential architectural designs.

10. One policy proposal resulting from choice theorists is _____ incapacitation of high-rate offenders.

11. Edward O. Wilson's studies in _____ attempted to explain _____ behavior as a _____ adaption.

12. _____ are people whose primitive impulses control their personality, often resulting in voices or visions.

13. Sigmund _____ is considered the father of psychoanalysis.

14. According to _____ _____ theory, children model their behavior after adults.

15. _____ is the absence or weakness of rules or social norms.

16. The social _____ theory holds the United States is a _____ society with unequal distribution of wealth, power and prestige.

17. According to Clifford R. Shaw and Henry D. McKay, the _____ neighborhood is an area in which important social _____ cannot function properly.

18 _____ is the frustration and anger members of the lower-class experience as a result of their inability to achieve social and financial _____ through legitimate avenues.

19. _____deprivation refers to the fact the economic burdens may go unnoticed where there is equivalent economic status.

20. Social _____ theorists believe the direction and quality of human interaction and relationships exert control over criminal behavior.

21. Victim _____ refers to the fact that many victims may have _____ the confrontation that led to their injury or death.

22. A _____ activities approach to criminal behavior suggests that criminal activity and victimization are related to the nature of everyday _____ of human behavior.

23. _____refers to the belief that dangerous criminal offenders should be locked away for _____ periods of time.

24. A recent variation of the strain theory is called _____ _____, where the burden of economic hardship might go unnoticed if all people shared an _____ economic status.

SELF TEST

True/False

25. Studies indicate that over the past two decades gang membership has been rising rapidly.

26. According to Cesare Beccaria and Jeremy Bentham, excessive force and punishment are effective crime deterrents.

27. One prominent view of criminality is that criminals are rational, weighing the potential benefits and/or consequences of their actions.

28. If general deterrence exists, there should be an inverse relationship between crime rates and the probability of sanctions.

29. "Gang homicide" is recognized as a separate and unique category of criminal behavior.

30. Researchers have failed to demonstrate that the death penalty deters murder.

31. Informal sanctions such as peer and parental disapproval are less powerful deterrents than criminal sanctions.

32. Situational crime prevention seeks changing criminals as opposed to changing environments so as to reduce opportunities for crime.

33. Nearly 70 percent of seventeen to twenty-two year-old parolees are rearrested within six years.

34. Hypoglycemia has been linked to violence and other antisocial behavior.

35. Inmates with mental disorders pose a greater risk to society upon release than does the typical inmate.

36. Violent media images clearly produces violent behavior among viewers.

37. The correctional system in Texas offers plastic surgery to inmates with physical deformities.

38. The lower-class subculture has norms in direct opposition to those of the middle-class.

39. According to learning theory, people are born "bad" but learn "good" through interacting with others.

40. According to theory of labeling, past criminal activity creates a stigma and leads one to be shunned by conventional society.

41. One view holds that where social differences are magnified by proximity between the affluent and the disadvantaged, higher crime results.

42. According to the life course view, events such as career establishment or marriage have little impact on criminal behavior.

43. Psychopaths are able to learn from their mistakes and to be deterred by punishment.

44. Control theory holds that all people may have the inclination to violate the law, but most are held in check by their relationship to conventional institutions and individuals such as the family, school, and peer group.

45. Conflict criminology focuses on the evils of capitalism and the free enterprise system.

46. According to NCVS data, most victimizations occur in public places, in rural areas, and during the evening.

MULTIPLE CHOICE

47.   Modern gangs rely on which of the following to encourage membership?

    a.   group loyalty
    b.   emotional involvement with neighborhood turf
    c.   drug profits and street power
    d.   none of the above

48.   Choice theorists believe crime results only after offenders consider which of the following:

    a.   personal need
    b.   situational factors
    c.   legal factors
    d.   none of the above

49.   According to inmate reports, which of the following is **not** a motivation for criminal activity.

    a.   to impress friends
    b.   to gain excitement
    c.   to provide for a family
    d.   to obtain money

50.   Which is **not** one of Ronald Clarke's crime prevention tactics.

    a.   increase the size of the police force
    b.   increase the risks of crime
    c.   reduce the rewards of crime
    d.   increase the effort needed to commit crime

51.   What percentage of prison inmates are considered to be psychopaths.

    a.   0 - 10
    b.   10 - 30
    c.   30 - 50
    d.   50 - 80

52. According to criminologists, which of the following statements relate to professional criminals.

a. identifies with a criminal subculture
b. makes the bulk of his or her living from crime
c. possesses a degree of skill in his or her chosen trade
d. all of the above

53. Which of the following is **not** associated with the social process theory.

a. self-control
b. learning
c. bond
d. strain

54. Hirschi's bond theory does **not** include which of the following:

a. attachment
b. appeal
c. belief
d. commitment

55. Which is **not** a branch of conflict theory.

a. peacemaking
b. radical feminism
c. left realism
d. all of the above are branches of the conflict theory

56. According to researchers Cohen and Felson, which of these factors would **not** explain predatory crime.

a. supply of motivated offenders
b. capitalism and free enterprise
c. supply of suitable targets
d. absence of effective guardians for protection

57. _____ deterrence is the belief that the pains of imprisonment should be so severe that upon release convicted offenders will not dare repeat their criminal acts.

    a. Special
    b. Perceptual
    c. General
    d. Effective

58. The origins of scientific criminology is usually traced to the research of which of the following researches.

    a. Henry D. McKay
    b. Edwin Sutherland
    c. Cesare Lombroso
    d. Raffaile Garofalo

59. People who are extremely anxious and fear that repressed unacceptable impulses may break through and control their behavior are _____.

    a. psychotics
    b. neurotics
    c. schizophrenics
    d. psychopaths

60. The effectiveness of general deterrence appears to be limited by which of the following

    a. the efficiency of the justice system
    b. the assumption of rational offenders
    c. the elaborate array of legal rights
    d. all of the above

61. Which of the following theorists is/are associated with the term anomie.

    a. Emile Durkheim
    b. Robert Merton
    c. Aldophe Quetlet
    d. both a and b

62.   Which criminologist is associated with the theory of differential association.

      a.   Edwin Sutherland
      b.   Walter Miller
      c.   Lloyd Ohlin
      d.   Robert Merton

63.   Which of the following **cannot** be classified as a learning theory.

      a.   neutralization
      b.   differential association
      c.   labeling
      d.   both a and b

MATCHING

64.   Control Theory   A.   Stigmatization

65.   Conflict Theory   B.   Differential association

66.   Learning Theory   C.   Stratified society

67.   Strain Theory   D.   Social bond

68.   Labeling Theory   E.   Alien Conspiracy Theory

69.   Social Structure Theory   F.   Anomie

ESSAY QUESTIONS

70.   Discuss several possible reasons for the failure of incapacitation to control crime.

71.   Are biological explanations for criminal acts valid. Why or why not.

72.   Discuss which of the psychological approaches to criminality you think best explains criminality, and why?

73.   Compare and contrast social structure theory with social process theory.

74.   Discuss the major premises of Differential Association theory; what does it appear to explain?

75.   Is the women's liberation movement responsible for increasing numbers of female offenders? Explain why, or why not, including some alternative causes.

76.   As more and more employed families lose their housing due to escalating rents, will crime increase? Is conflict theory important and valid in explaining criminality?

77.   If crime is considered to be a routine activity, what steps can be taken to avoid becoming a crime victim?

CHAPTER THREE ANSWER SECTION

FILL-IN REVIEW

1   fifty
2   Psychological
3.   genetic, neurological
4.   choice, benefits, consequences
5.   everyone, conventional, criminal
6.   swift, certain, severe
7.   rational
8.   Specific, repeat
9.   defensible
10.   selective
11.   sociobiology, social, genetic
12.   Psychotics
13.   Freud
14.   social learning
15.   Anomie
16.   structure, stratified
17.   disorganized, institutions
18.   Strain, success
19.   Relative
20.   process
21.   precipitation, initiated
22.   routine, patterns
23.   Incapacitation, long
24.   relative deprivation, equivalent

SELF TEST

True/False

25.	T	36.	F
26.	F	37.	T
27.	T	38.	T
28.	T	39.	F
29.	T	40.	T
30.	T	41.	T
31.	F	42.	T
32.	F	43.	F
33.	T	44.	T
34.	T	45.	F
35.	F	46.	F

MULTIPLE CHOICE

47.	C	56.	B
48.	D	57.	A
49.	C	58.	C
50.	A	59.	B
51.	B	60.	D
52.	D	61.	D
53.	D	62.	A
54.	B	63.	C
55.	D		

MATCHING

64.	D
65.	E
66.	B
67.	F
68.	A
69.	C

4   Criminal Law: Substance and Procedure

LEARNING OBJECTIVES

1. Explain the meaning of substantive criminal law and procedural law.

2. Define the legal principle of *stare decisis*.

3. Describe the historical development of common law into statute.

4. Differentiate between criminal law and civil law.

5. Discuss the purposes of the criminal law.

6. Distinguish between a felony and a misdemeanor.

7. Discuss the legal definition of a crime.

8. Define the elements which constitute the *corpus delicti* of a crime.

9. Describe several major criminal defenses.

10. Discuss the role of the Constitution and Bill of Rights in criminal law.

CHAPTER SUMMARY

The law that defines criminal behavior in the United States is known as **substantive criminal law**. **Procedural law** consists of the rules designed to implement substantive law which governs the processing of criminal suspects and the conduct of criminal trials. Each state government, as well as the federal government, has its own criminal code that has been developed over many generations. American criminal law is based on the **British common law** system and incorporates moral, social, political and economic concerns.

In modern society, law can be divided into two broad categories: criminal law and civil law. In **criminal law**, the major objective is to protect the public against harm by preventing the commission of criminal offenses; primary emphasis is on the intent of the individual committing the crime. In **civil law**, the major concern is that the injured party be compensated for any harm done; primary attention is given to affixing the blame each party deserves for producing the damage or conflict. The criminal law serves a number of purposes. It identifies public wrongs, exerts social control, deters anti-social behavior, regulates punishments and maintains the social order.

A **crime** can be defined as (1) a legal wrong (2) prohibited by the criminal law (3) prosecuted by the state (4) in a formal court proceeding (5) in which a criminal sanction or sentence may be imposed. The classification of crime that is most common in the United States is the **felony-misdemeanor** breakdown, based on the seriousness of the nature of the crime. The elements that make up a crime, known as the **corpus delicti**, include: the **actus reus,** the **mens rea**, and the combination of actus reus and mens rea. **Actus reus**, which literally translates as the "guilty act," refers to the forbidden act itself and is used to describe the physical crime and/or the commission of the criminal act. **Mens rea**, which literally translates as the "guilty mind," deals with the intent to commit a criminal act. To constitute a criminal act, there must be a **concurrence** or combination of **both** the act and the intent.

Under the criminal law, adults are presumed to realize the consequences of their actions, but the law does not hold an individual blameworthy unless that person is capable of **intending** to commit the crime as accused. Such factors as insanity, a mental defect, intoxication, or age, mitigate a person's criminal responsibility. There are also criminal defenses based on the concept of justification or excuse. These include: consent, self-defense, entrapment, double jeopardy, mistake, compulsion, and necessity.

The **Bill of Rights** of the U.S. Constitution provides some fundamental rights and protections for citizens, and specifically, criminal defendants. The **Fourth Amendment** limits police search and seizure abilities requiring warrants based on probable cause and establishes a privacy right. The **Fifth Amendment** provides for rights against double jeopardy and self-incrimination and ensures **due process**. The **Sixth Amendment** guarantees a speedy, public trial before an impartial jury and the right to counsel and to confront witnesses. The **Eighth Amendment** protects against excessive bail and cruel and unusual punishment. Because of the theory of **selective incorporation**, rights found to be fundamental and implicit to the U.S. justice system have been incorporated on a case-by-case basis, through application of the **Fourteenth Amendment**, to apply to the states.

Criminal Law: Substance and Procedure

KEY TERMS AND CONCEPTS

Substantive Criminal Law
Criminal Procedure
Procedural Law
Civil Law
Torts
Intent
Common Law
Law of Precedent
Stare Decisis
Ex Post Facto Laws
Bills of Attainder
Substantive Due Process
Felony
Misdemeanor
In-Presence Requirement
Corpus Delicti
Actus Reus
Carriers Case
Statute
Crime
Administrative Rules
Infraction
Fourth Amendment
Fifth Amendment
Sixth Amendment

Mens Rea
Criminal Negligence
Specific Intent
Strict Liability
Insanity
M'Naghten Rule
Irresistible Impulse Test
Durham Rule
Products Test
Substantial Capacity Test
Appreciation Test
Entrapment
RICO
Preventive Detention
Separation of Powers
Bill of Rights
Double Jeopardy
Mores
Inchoate Offenses
Fundamental Faimes
Due Process
Crime of Omission
Powell v. Texas
Fourteenth Amendment
Eighth Amendment

FILL-IN REVIEW

1. _____ _____ law that regulates conduct in our society.

2. _____ law involves the rules designed to implement the substantive law.

3. Development of formal law in the original colonies was adopted from _____ _____ law.

4. _____ requires that a judicial decision is generally binding on courts in subsequent applicable cases; this legal principle is known as _____ _____.

5. In _____ law, the state initiates the legal process and can impose _____ .

6. In _____ law, the major concern is that the injured party be _____ for any harm done.

39

Chapter 4

7. A _____ is a civil or private wrong.

8. In criminal law, the emphasis is on the _____ of the individual to commit a crime.

9. The Constitution forbids _____ _____ _____ laws, which create crimes and penalties that can be enforced retroactively.

10. The Constitution forbids _____ _____which are legislative acts that inflict punishment without a judicial trial.

11. The Constitution has been interpreted to forbid any criminal law which violates a person's right to be treated fairly and equally. This is known as _____ _____ process.

12. The difference between a _____ and a _____ is based primarily on the seriousness of the crime.

13. The _____ - _____ _____means, under normal circumstances, that unless a police officer directly observes a misdemeanor take place, the officer cannot make an arrest.

14. The term _____ _____ is used to describe all of the elements which together constitute a crime.

15. The physical act of a crime is the _____ _____, whereas the intent to commit a crime is the _____ _____.

16. There are certain statutory offenses where mens rea is not essential. These offenses are known as _____ _____ crimes.

16. If a person is found to be insane at the time they committed a criminal act, a judgment of _____ _____by reason of _____ is entered.

18. The M'Naghten Rule is known as the _____ - _____test.

19. The _____ _____ test excuses people from criminal responsibility when they might be able to distinguish between right and wrong, but their mental condition impairs their ability to control themselves.

20. The Durham Rule for determining criminal insanity is also called the _____ test.

21. The _____ _____ test, which is becoming increasingly popular with many courts, is basically a broader restatement of the M'Naughten rule-irresistable impulse test.

22.   The federal government uses an _____ _____ with regard to insanity pleas.

23.   In order to claim a not guilty plea by reason of _____ -_____, the defendant must have acted under a reasonable belief that he or she was in imminent danger of death or great personal harm and had no escape or retreat possible.

24.   A defense based on _____ excuses a defendant from criminal liability when police use traps, decoys, and deception to induce criminal action.

25.   _____ or _____ of the law is generally no defense to a crime.

26.   _____ _____ allows judges to detain offenders in jail prior to their trials if they are considered a danger to the community and/or themselves.

27.   In 1791, the _____ of _____ was added to the Constitution to prevent any future government from usurping the personal freedoms of citizens.

28.   The police can search and seize evidence under certain circumstances with a properly authorized _____ _____, based on _____ _____.

29.   The _____ Amendment includes the right to privacy.

30.   The right of people to be treated fairly and openly when they are confronted by the state authority is known as _____ _____ of law.

31.   The theory of _____ _____ states that the Bill of Rights does not apply to the states through the due process clause of the _____ Amendment, but only on a case-by-case basis.

SELF TEST

True/False

32.   The criminal law is constantly evolving to keep pace with society and its changing needs.

33.   American law has been adopted primarily from the French common law system.

34.   The combination of actus reus and mens rea is an integral part of the corpus delicti.

35.   A tort is a private wrong, and is part of civil law.

Chapter 4

36. A felony can be distinguished from a misdemeanor in that the latter is punishable by fine or imprisonment other than in a penitentiary.

37. The in-presence requirement makes it necessary for a police officer to be present, when either a felony or misdemeanor has been committed, in order to make an arrest.

38. A strict liability offense does not require concurrence of act and intent.

39. The Constitution forbids government passage of ex post facto laws.

40. The Durham Rule basically states that an accused is not criminally responsible if his unlawful act was the product of mental disease of defect.

41. In criminal law the emphasis is on affixing the blame each party deserves for producing the damage or conflict.

42. Voluntary intoxication can never mitigate the degree of a crime.

43. Self-defense cannot be used in the defense of another or the defense of one's property.

44. As a general rule, the consent of a victim to a crime does not justify or excuse the defendant who commits the action.

45. The double jeopardy clause of the Constitution does not allow a defendant to be re-tried if the first trial ended in a hung jury.

46. There are specific statutes against organized crime.

47. The purpose of the separation of powers in the Constitution was written to ensure that no single branch of the government could usurp power for itself and institute dictatorship.

48. The Eighth Amendment guarantees a constitutional right to bail.

49. The first ten amendments and the Fourteenth Amendment are commonly referred to as the Bill of Rights.

50. The Fourteenth Amendment's due process clause does **not** apply to state governments.

51. The sixth amendment to the United States constitution provides for traditional limits on police behavior.

52. The Brady Handgun Control Law of 1993 requires a five-business-day waiting period before an individual can purchase a handgun.

MULTIPLE CHOICE

53. Which of the following is **not** a purpose of the criminal law.

    a.   maintains social order
    b.   exerts social control
    c.   provides compensation to individuals for harm done
    d.   regulates punishments

54. Which of the following is **not** a misdemeanor.

    a.   larceny
    b.   assault and battery
    c.   robbery
    d.   unlawful possession of marijuana

55. Which of the following is **not** a strict liability criminal statute.

    a.   narcotics control laws
    b.   traffic laws
    c.   sanitation laws
    d.   white collar crime control laws

56. The primary test for criminal responsibility in the United States is the:

    a.   M'Naghten Rule
    b.   Substantial Capacity Test
    c.   Durham Rule
    d.   none of the above

57. The corpus delicti includes:

    a.   the actus reus
    b.   the mens rea
    c.   the combination of the actus reus and mens rea
    d.   all of the above

58. The _____law involves the use of rules designed to implement the substantive criminal law.

    a.   common
    b.   procedural
    c.   precedent
    d.   civil

59.   Which of the following is **not** a similarity between criminal and civil law.

    a.   both seek to control behavior
    b.   both impose sanctions
    c.   both place emphasis on the intent of the individual committing the crime
    d.   all of the above are similarities of criminal and civil law.

60.   The basic elements required to constitute a crime are known as the:

    a.   actus reus
    b.   mens reus
    c.   corpus delicti
    d.   intent

61.   Criminal statutes that do not require the proof of criminal intent, or mens rea, are:

    a.   private welfare crimes
    b.   strict liability crimes
    c.   mala in se crimes
    d.   both a and b

62.   The Durham Rule is also known as the:

    a.   products test
    b.   right-wrong test
    c.   substantial capacity test
    d.   impulse test

63.   When a decision is made by a court, that decision is generally binding in similar courts in subsequent applicable cases. This is known as:

    a.   stare decisis
    b.   law of precedent
    c.   procedural law
    d.   both a and b

64.   The M'Naghten Rule has been supplemented with the _____ _____ test in many states where it is used.

    a.   irresistible impulse
    b.   diminished capacity
    c.   substantial capacity
    d.   both a and c

65.   A child under the age of _____ cannot be held criminally responsible.

    a.   5
    b.   7
    c.   14
    d.   16

66.   Consent would **not** be an appropriate defense for:

    a.   larceny/theft
    b.   common law rape
    c.   assaults
    d.   none of the above

67.   Which of the following offenses are **not** listed under RICO.

    a.   murder
    b.   rape
    c.   arson
    d.   bribery

68.   The Fourth Amendment includes the:

    a.   right to privacy
    b.   right against self-incrimination
    c.   right to a speedy and public trial
    d.   prohibition of cruel and unusual punishment

69.   The Fifth Amendment includes the:

    a.   right to privacy
    b.   right against self-incrimination
    c.   right to a speedy and public trial
    d.   prohibition of cruel and unusual punishment

70.   The Sixth Amendment includes the:

    a.   right to privacy
    b.   right against self-incrimination
    c.   right to a speedy and public trial
    d.   prohibition of cruel and unusual punishment

71.   The Eighth Amendment includes the:

        a.   right to privacy
        b.   right against self-incrimination
        c.   right to a speedy and public trial
        d.   prohibition of cruel and unusual punishment

72.   Which of the following are **not** considered a due process procedural safeguard for
        the offender.

        a.   notices of charges
        b.   an informal hearing
        c.   the right to counsel
        d.   the opportunity to present one's own witnesses

73.   Which of the following is **not** a source of criminal law.

        a.   statutes
        b.   case decisions
        c.   constitutional laws
        d.   all of the above are sources of criminal law

74.   Which of the following is forbidden by the Constitution.

        a.   making a person's status a crime
        b.   bills of attainder
        c.   creating crimes that can be retroactively enforced
        d.   all of the above

75.   Which of the following Justices is the newest member of the United States Supreme Court.

        a.   Stephen Breyer
        b.   Ruth Bader Ginsburg
        c.   Clarence Thomas
        d.   Harry Blackmun

MATCHING

76.	Procedural Law	A.	The "body of crime"
77.	M'Naghten Rule	B.	The "guilty mind"
78.	Corpus delicti	C.	implements criminal law
79.	Civil Law	D.	Irresistible Impulse Test
80.	Mens rea	E.	Private Wrongs
81.	Durham Rule	F.	The "guilty act"
82.	Actus reus	G.	Products Test
83.	Common Law	H.	source of substantive law

ESSAY QUESTIONS

84. Discuss the influence of British common law on our criminal law system today.

85. Describe five major purposes of the criminal law.

86. Briefly discuss the major classifications of crime.

87. In recent years, numerous states have revised their penal codes. What are some of the major categories of substantive crimes you think should be revised? Why?

88. Discuss the elements that constitute the corpus delicti of a crime.

89. Describe the similarities and differences between the criminal and civil law. Which would you rather be tried under? Why?

90. Briefly discuss the five major types of criminal defenses regarding justification or excuse. Do you agree or disagree with each defense?

91. What are the minimum standards of procedure required in the criminal justice system?

92. Discuss the relationship between the U.S. Constitution and the Bill of Rights. What particular provisions does the incorporation theory involve?

CHAPTER FOUR ANSWER SECTION

FILL-IN REVIEW

1. Substantive criminal
2. Procedural
3. British common
4. Precedent, stare decisis
5. criminal, sanctions
6. civil, compensated
7. tort
8. intent
9. ex post facto
10. bills of attainder
11. substantive due
12. felony, misdemeanor
13. in-presence requirement
14. corpus delicti
15. actus reus, mens rea
16. strict liability
17. not guilty, insanity
18. right-wrong
19. irresistible impulse
20. products
21. substantial capacity
22. appreciation test
23. self-defense
24. entrapment
25. Mistake, ignorance
26. Preventive detention
27. Bill of Rights
28. search warrant, probable cause
29. Fourth
30. due process
31. selective incorporation, Fourteenth

SELF TEST

True/False

32.	T	43.	F
33.	F	44.	T
34.	T	45.	F
35.	T	46.	F
36.	T	47.	T
37.	F	48.	F
38.	T	49.	T
39.	T	50.	F
40.	T	51.	F
41.	F	52.	T
42.	F		

MULTIPLE CHOICE

53.	C	65.	B
54.	C	66.	C
55.	D	67.	B
56.	A	68.	A
57.	D	69.	B
58.	B	70.	C
59.	C	71.	D
60.	C	72.	B
61.	B	73.	D
62.	A	74.	D
63.	D	75.	A
64.	A		

MATCHING

76.	C
77.	D
78.	A
79.	E
80.	B
81.	G
82.	F
83.	H

5   Police in Society: History and Organization

LEARNING OBJECTIVES

1.   Describe the significance of the pledge system, the watch system, a tithing, and a shire.

2.   Explain the significance of Sir Robert Peel.

3.   Discuss the early police departments and the role that politics had in them.

4.   Discuss the reform of the police departments in the twentieth century. Explain the significance of August Vollmer.

5.   Describe the period of policing between the years 1960 to 1990.

6.   Differentiate between the functions of metropolitan, county, and state police agencies.

7.   Discuss the role of at least two federal agencies under the jurisdiction of the Justice Department and the Treasury Department.

8.   Discuss the changes we can expect to see in law enforcement in the future.

9.   Describe several of the recent technological advances with respect to policing and criminal justice.

10.   Differentiate between private security and sworn public police officers.

CHAPTER SUMMARY

As was the case with the criminal law, the origin of the United States police agencies can be traced back to early English society. Before the Norman conquest, there was no English police and every person was responsible for aiding neighbors in crime-related problems. This was known as the **pledge** system. Ten **tithings** were grouped into a **hundred** and were supervised by a constable, who could be considered the police officer. **Shires**, which resemble the counties of today, were controlled by the **shire reeve** who was appointed by the crown or local landowner to supervise the territory and ensure that order would be kept. The shire reeve, forerunner of today's **sheriff**, soon began to pursue and apprehend law violators as part of his duties. Various forms of policing evolved until the eighteenth century, when in 1829, under **Sir Robert Peel**, the first police department was formed in London and proved so successful that by 1856 every borough and county in England was required to form its own police force.

The modern police department was born out of urban mob violence in the nation's cities in the nineteenth century. Boston created the first formal U.S. police department in 1838. During this time, politics dominated the departments and determined the recruitment of new officers and promotion of supervisors. Police during the nineteenth century were generally incompetent, corrupt, and disliked by the people they served. In an effort to control police corruption, civic leaders in a number of jurisdictions created police administrative boards to reduce the control local officials exercised over police. Police professionalism grew in the early part of the twentieth century, stressing incorruptible, tough, highly trained, rule-oriented law enforcement departments, organized along militaristic lines. During the 1960's and 1970's, police work became highly scrutinized and underwent a period of civil unrest, producing tension between police and the public. Thus, in the 1980's, the relationship between the police and the community took on even more importance.

There are approximately 17,000 law enforcement agencies in the United States employing more than 830,000 people including 630,000 sworn officers and about 250,000 civilians. City police comprise the majority of the nation's authorized law enforcement personnel. Patrol officers spend a great deal of time in areas other than crime fighting, including: traffic enforcement, emergency medical care, jail operation, crowd control, and other community services.

The **U.S. Department of Justice** is the legal arm of the United States Government. Headed by the attorney general, it is empowered to enforce federal laws, represent the United States when it is party to court action, and conduct independent investigations through its law enforcement services. One branch of the Department of Justice is the **Federal Bureau of Investigation** (FBI), an investigative agency with jurisdiction over all matters in which the United States is, or may be, an interested party. It limits its jurisdiction to federal laws including all federal statutes not specifically assigned to other agencies. The **Drug Enforcement Administration** (DEA) is an agency which assists local and state authorities in their investigation of illegal drug use and carries out independent surveillance and enforcement activities to control the importation of narcotics. Other federal law enforcement agencies under the direction of the Justice Department include the **U.S. Marshals**, the **Immigration and Naturalization Service** (INS), and the **Organized Crime and Racketeering Unit**. The U.S. Treasury Department maintains the following enforcement branches: the **Bureau of Alcohol, Tobacco, and Firearms** (ATF), the **Internal Revenue Service** (IRS), the **Customs Bureau**, and the **Secret Service**.

Police departments in the future are looking toward reshaping their role by placing greater emphasis on **community oriented policing**. (COR). This strategy involves deemphasizing crime fighting and stressing community organization and revitalization. Police departments utilizing this technique are increasing the numbers of female and minority police officers as well as the number of civilian employees. Community-oriented policing relies on decentralization, efficiency and a proactive approach to crime fighting. A further trend will be the reliance on technology to improve effectiveness of police resources. This technology involves the use of computers to identify criminals, DNA profiling, fingerprint identification, and teleconferencing.

The emergence of the private security industry has been dramatic, increasing at a much greater pace than public policing. Private security can be categorized into two main groups. **Propriety security** is undertaken by an organization's own employees and includes both plainclothes and uniformed agents directed by the organization's head of security. The second type of private security are **contractual services** such as guards, investigators, armored cars, and so on which are provided by private companies. Private security officers enjoy more legal leeway than public police and are not subject to criminal and/or civil damages for false arrests, although their organizations are responsible for other inappropriate behaviors such as brutality and/or shootings. The Hallcrest Report has suggested several steps which might improve private security, including mandatory training and statewide regulatory agencies.

KEY TERMS AND CONCEPTS

Pledge System	O.W. Wilson
Tithing	Sheriff
Hue and Cry	State Police
Constable	U.S. Department of Justice
Shires	Federal Bureau of Investigation (FBI)
Viglante Thief Takers	Drug Enforcement Administration (DEA)
Shire Reeve	U.S Treasury Department
Watch System	DNA Profiling
Sir Robert Peel	Teleconferencing
August Vollmer	Proprietary Security
Hallcrest Report	International Association of Chiefs of Police
Contractual Services	Decentralization
Community Oriented Policing (COP)	

FILL-IN REVIEW

1.   In early England, people were grouped in a collective of _____ families, called a _____, and entrusted with policing their own minor problems.

2.   Ten tithings were grouped into a hundred, whose affairs were supervised by a _____ .

3.   In the thirteenth century, the _____ system was created to help protect property in England's larger cities and towns.

Police in Society: History and Organization

4. _____ created the first formal U.S. police department in 1838; the new departments replaced the _____ - _____ system.

5. The first organized police force was established in London in 1829 by Sir_____ _____.

6. While serving as police chief of Berkeley, California, August Vollmer instituted _____ training as an important part of the development of young officers.

7. During the 1960's, the _____ _____ movement produced a growing tension between citizens who were demanding increased rights and freedoms, and the police, whose role often became focused on security and maintaining the status quo.

8. The 1970's saw increased recruitment of _____ and _____ police officers.

9. There are approximately _____ law enforcement agencies in the United States.

10. Most of the nation's county law enforcement departments are independent agencies whose senior officer, the _____, is usually an _____ political official.

11. _____ police comprise the majority of the nation's authorized law enforcement_____.

12. _____ police were legislatively created to deal with growing incidence of crime in _____ areas, a consequence of the increase in population mobility.

13. The Department of _____ is the legal arm of the United States Government.

14. Agents of the _____ _____ _____ assist local and state authorities in their investigation of illegal drug use and carry out independent surveillance and enforcement activities to control importation of narcotics.

15. The _____ _____ is an arm of the Treasury Department, and was originally charged with enforcing laws against counterfeiting.

16. Private security companies which provide guards, investigators, armored cars, and so on are referred to as _____ services.

17. The _____ Commission was created by President Herbert Hoover and conducted a national study of criminal justice.

18. The decade of the _____ saw the advent of sensitivity training, community advisory boards, public service officers and special services.

19. _____ residents tend to have higher esteem for police.

20. Most sheriff's departments are _____ offices, and any change in form or duties would require an amendment.

21. The _____ Report was a government financed study of the _____ security industry.

SELF TEST

True/False

22. Under the pledge system, people were grouped in a collective of families called a shire.

23. Vigilantes were social crusaders who believed in nonviolent methods for dealing with offenders.

24. In New York, the police were responsible for street-sweeping until the late 1800's.

25. Police during the nineteenth century were generally competent, honest, and well liked by the people they served.

26. The first police car was used in New York City in the early 1900's.

27. O.W. Wilson was instrumental in applying modern management and administrative techniques to policing.

28. The duties of a county sheriff's department vary according to the size and development of the county in which it is seated.

29. Decentralization of command is believed to increase sensitivity to citizen needs and create special knowledge of an area.

30. The Secret Service is an arm of the U.S. Justice Department.

31. The computer is currently being utilized in fingerprint identification.

32. Today, there are more sworn public police officers than there are private security officers.

33. Private security officers are given less legal leeway than local public police officers.

34. Under Sir Robert Peel, the London police force was structured much like the military.

35.   Colonial sheriffs were salaried on a fee system related to their effectiveness, receiving a fixed amount for every arrest made, for taxes collected and for summonses served.

36.   Between 1920 and 1960, the majority of police officers had an aggressive style of policing.

37.   The Law Enforcement Assistance Administration (LEAA) provided federal funds to police agencies.

38.   The majority of police departments in America have less than fifty officers and serve a population of under 25,000.

39.   May state police agencies direct their attention to traffic law enforcement.

40.   In general, State Supreme Courts and Federal Appellate Courts have ruled that DNA evidence is a violation of the Fourth Amendment privacy right.

41.   Police moonlighting creates liability and conflict of interest issues.

MULTIPLE CHOICE

42.   The origin of U.S. police agencies can be traced back to early
      _____ society.

      a.   German
      b.   Irish
      c.   English
      d.   Italian

43.   In what year did Sir Robert Peel establish the London police force.

      a.   1776
      b.   1796
      c.   1829
      d.   1859

44.   The first formal police department in the United States was developed in which city:

      a.   New York
      b.   Philadelphia
      c.   Baltimore
      d.   Boston

Chapter 5

45. Hundreds came together to compose _____, which resemble counties of today.

    a. shires
    b. shire-reeves
    c. tithings
    d. both a and b

46. The reason(s) for the turmoil and crisis the police endured in the 1960's and 1970's can be attributed to which of the following:

    a. social problems
    b. Supreme Court rulings
    c. rapidly growing crime rate
    d. all of the above

47. There are approximately 17,000 law enforcement agencies in the U.S. which employ approximately _____ sworn officers.

    a. 48,000
    b. 190,000
    c. 380,000
    d. 620,000

48. Which of the following is **not** a duty of the sheriff's department.

    a. court security
    b. operating the county jail
    c. coroners' investigations
    d. all of the above are duties of a sheriff's department

49. About 23 _____ agencies have the same general police powers as municipal police and are limited only by their _____ boundaries.

    a. military police, county
    b. state police, state
    c. county sheriff, county
    d. immigration services, country

50. Which is the legal arm of the United States government.

    a. U.S. Justice Department
    b. U.S. Treasury Department
    c. U.S. Immigration Department
    d. U.S. Customs Department

51.   Which of the following is **not** under the FBI's jurisdiction.

    a.   espionage
    b.   treason
    c.   counterfeiting
    d.   mail fraud

52.   The Bureau of Alcohol, Tobacco, and Firearms falls under the _____ Department.

    a.   Justice
    b.   Treasury
    c.   Customs
    d.   Defense

53.   Through the use of DNA profiling, a DNA match indicates there is a _____ to one chance the suspect is **not** the offender.

    a.   10,000
    b.   100,000
    c.   1 million
    d.   no statistical estimate of accuracy need be reported

54.   The term _____ refers to efforts undertaken by a private organization using their own employees, and including both plain clothes and uniformed agents.

    a.   propriety security
    b.   contractual security
    c.   vigilante security
    d.   structured security

55.   Which is/are major problem(s) confronting the police.

    a.   a greater number of criminals
    b.   shrinking budgets and resources
    c.   technological changes
    d.   all of the above are major problems confronting the police

56.   Approximately _____ states have privatized some of their police functions.

    a.   5
    b.   15
    c.   20
    d.   25

57. Approximately _____ percent of police departments prohibit moonlighting.

    a.   20
    b.   40
    c.   60
    d.   75

58. The Hallcrest Report recommended which of the following to improve private security.

    a.   upgrading employee quality
    b.   creating statewide regulatory agencies
    c.   mandatory training
    d.   all of the above were recommendations of the Hallcrest Report

59. Which of the following are likely future trends in policing.

    a.   decentralization
    b.   increased civilian employment
    c.   greater technology applied to crime investigation
    d.   all of the above are likely future trends

MATCHING

60.	Tithing	A.	Elected official
61.	Sir Robert Peel	B.	University training
62.	August Vollmer	C.	Treasury Department
63.	Sheriff	D.	Computers
64.	DEA	E.	Ten families
65.	Customs Bureau	F.	Private security
66.	Fingerprint analysis	G.	U.S. Department of Justice
67.	Contractual services	H.	First organized police force in London

ESSAY QUESTIONS

68. Differentiate between the roles and duties of the state police, sheriffs, and local police departments.

69. Briefly discuss the federal law enforcement agencies and their functions.

70. What factors have contributed to the growth of the private security industry? What factors will influence the private security industry in the coming decade?

71. Describe several of the technological advances which police should use in solving more crimes more efficiently. What are the possible dangers of using these technologies?

72. Discuss the trends which will influence policing in the future. Discuss what other social factors may impact policing in the 21st century.

CHAPTER FIVE ANSWER SECTION

FILL-IN REVIEW

1. ten, tithing
2. Constable
3. watch
4. Boston, night-watch
5. Robert Peel
6. university
7. Civil Rights
8. women, minority
9. 17,000
10. Sheriff, elected
11. City, personnel
12. State, nonurban
13. Justice
14. Drug Enforcement Administration
15. Secret Service
16. contractual
17. Wickersham
18. 1970s
19. Rural
20. constitutional
21. Hallcrest, private

SELF TEST

True/False

22.	F	32.	F
23.	F	33.	F
24.	T	34.	T
25.	F	35.	T
26.	F	36.	F
27.	T	37.	T
28.	T	38.	T
29.	T	39.	T
30.	F	40.	F
31.	T	41.	T

MULTIPLE CHOICE

42.	C		51.	C
43.	C		52.	B
44.	D		53.	D
45.	A		54.	A
46.	D		55.	B
47.	D		56.	C
48.	D		57.	B
49.	B		58.	D
50.	A		59.	D

MATCHING

60.	E
61.	H
62.	B
63.	A
64.	G
65.	C
66.	D
67.	F

6   The Police: Organization, Role, and Function

LEARNING OBJECTIVES

1. Describe several specialized units a metropolitan police department is likely to have.

2. Describe the structural organization of a typical police department.

3. Discuss the various activities patrol officers engage in.

4. Discuss the proactive versus the reactive approach to crime fighting.

5. Discuss the investigation function.

6. Describe the concept and effectiveness of Community Oriented Policing (COP), and Problem-Oriented Policing (POP).

7. Detail the support and administrative functions of police departments and their contributions toward improving the quality of policing.

8. Compare and contrast the types of criteria used for recruit selection and their value in predicting job performance.

9. Define police productivity and the techniques used to accomplish it.

CHAPTER SUMMARY

Most police departments are independent agencies, operating without specific administrative control from any higher governmental authority, organized hierarchically. Most departments employ a **time-in-rank** system for determining promotion. Under this approach, an officer must spend a certain amount of time in the next lowest rank before he or she can be considered for advancement.

The Police: Organization, Role, and Function

Patrol officers are the backbone of the police department, accounting for about 60 percent of a department's personnel. Patrol officers are charged with supervising specific areas of their jurisdiction, called **beats**, whether it be on foot, in a patrol car, or by motorcycle, horse, helicopter, plane or boat. The greatest bulk of police patrol efforts are devoted to what has been described as **order maintenance**, or **peacekeeping**. An evaluation of the effectiveness of patrol was measured by the **Kansas City** study which indicated that variations in patrol techniques had little effect on crime. It was discovered that increasing the number of patrol cars in a beat did not reduce crime, fear of crime, or enhance citizen satisfaction with the police. The results from the study set the stage for a change in the manner in which tasks were approached, prompting the success of **proactive** patrol. A proactive approach to crime fighting requires officers to initiate actions against law violators. The downside of aggressive tactics is resentment of minority communities. Such proactive approaches have been shown to have deterrent effects in cases of domestic violence. One major study, however, concluded that adding police officers had little impact on the crime rate.

Police departments have **detectives** on staff who are experienced civil servants trained in investigatory techniques. Detectives are considered the elite of the police force: they are usually paid more than patrol officers, engage in interesting tasks, wear civilian clothes, and are subject to less stringent departmental control than patrol officers. Detective divisions are typically organized into bureaus such as homicide, robbery, or rape. Criticism has been leveled at the nation's detective forces for being bogged down in paperwork and being relatively inefficient at clearing cases. The Rand study found that a great deal of a detective's time was spent in nonproductive work and that investigative expertise did little to solve cases; the researchers estimated that one-half of all detectives could be replaced without negatively influencing crime clearance rates.

Police-community relations (PCR) programs have developed in an effort to make citizens more aware of police activities, alert them to methods of self-protection, and improve general attitudes toward policing. Kelling and Wilson articulated the "broken windows" approach in an attempt to improve police-community relations. They contend that the core police role must be altered to gain community involvement and citizen cooperation. One important goal of **community oriented policing** is to reduce the level of **fear** in the community. **Decentralization** and a "bottom-up" approach to dealing with community problems are essential elements in community policing. **Problem-oriented policing** is closely associated, and requires police agencies to identify particular long-term community problems and help develop strategies for their elimination.

A large part of police resources is devoted to support and administrative functions, including: personnel services; internal affairs; budget and finance; records and communications; training; community relations; crime prevention; laboratory; planning and research; property; and detention.

The civil service system has removed much of the politics from policing. Candidate selection generally includes: Written tests, oral interviews, psychological evaluations, physical fitness examinations and background checks. More than half of the nations police departments employ polygraphs and over sixty percent employ individual or group simulations as part of the selection process.

Chapter 6

Police productivity refers to the amount of actual order, maintenance, crime control, and other activities provided by individual police officers, and concomitantly, by police departments as a whole. **Consolidation** of police services combines small departments, usually with less than ten employees, in adjoining areas into a super-agency that services the previously fragmented jurisdictions. Some of the techniques used to accomplish this include: informal arrangements, sharing, pooling, contracting, civilian employees, multiple-tasking, and budget supplementation.

KEY TERMS AND CONCEPTS

Detective Bureau
Time-In Rank
Order Maintenance
Peacekeeping
Kansas City Study
Detection
Sting Operations
Proactive
Police-Community Relations (PCR)
Team Policing
Reactive
Decentralization
Pooling
Contracting
Investigation
Personality Tests
Job-Related Tests
Selective Enforcement

Broken Windows
Foot Patrol
Community Oriented Policing
Problem-Oriented Policing
"Hot Spots" of Crime
Participatory Management
Police Productivity
Internal Affairs
Consolidation
Multiple-tasks
Selective Enforcement
Budget Supplementation
Differential Police Response
Domestic Violence
Kansas City Gun Experiment
Police Service Districts
Physical Agility Tests
Special needs population

FILL-IN REVIEW

1. _____ _____ are the backbone of the police department, usually accounting for about _____ percent of a department's personnel.

2. Patrol officers are charged with supervising specific areas of their jurisdiction, which is known as a _____.

3. Most experts today agree that the bulk of police patrol efforts are devoted to _____ maintenance or _____ functions.

4. Data from the _____ _____ study indicated that variations in _____ techniques had little effect on crime patterns.

5. A _____ approach to crime fighting requires officers to initiate actions against law violators.

64

The Police: Organization, Role, and Function

6.   In regard to undercover work, _____ operations involve organized groups of _____ who deceive criminals into openly committing _____ acts or conspiring to engage in criminal activity.

7.   Efforts have been directed at improving the relationships between police departments and the public through programs known as _____ - _____ relations.

8.   A patrol strategy that focuses on community structure and needs rather than crime fighting is known as the _____ _____ approach.

9.   Identifying particular _____ problems and developing strategies to counteract them is known as _____ - _____ policing.

10.   A branch of a larger police department which is charged with "policing the police" is known as _____ _____ .

11.   _____ _____ refers to the amount of actual order maintenance, crime control, and other activities provided by individual police officers, and concomitantly by police departments as a whole.

12.   _____ - _____ involves training police officers to carry out other functions of municipal government.

13.   _____ of small departments results in a super agency to service previously fragmented jurisdictions.

14.   Handling incidents in an informal, noncriminal manner is referred to as _____ _____ .

15.   Crackdowns on criminal activities can result in _____, whereby criminals move to less well-protected areas.

16.   Decisions made by officers on the scene, rather than directives from headquarters, is referred to as a _____ - _____ approach.

17.   _____ police action (such as arrest) may have a _____ deterrent effect.

18.   The _____ _____ _____ Experiment, which directed efforts as restricting the carrying of guns at high-risk times in high-risk places, saw a decrease of almost _____ percent in gun crimes.

19.   In the Minneapolis Domestic Violence survey, it was found that after 6 months, only _____ percent of those arrested repeated their violent behavior.

Chapter 6

SELF TEST

True/False

20. Most American municipal departments are independent agencies, operating **without** specific administrative control from higher governmental authority.

21. Most research efforts show that a police officer's crime-fighting efforts are the major part of his or her overall activities.

22. Order maintenance functions fall on the borderline between criminal and non-criminal behavior.

23. Research data by Sherman and Berk indicates that when police took formal action (arrest) in domestic violence cases, that the chance of recidivism was substantially less than when the police took less punitive measures.

24. Research efforts have found that the actual number of law enforcement officers in a jurisdiction had a major impact on the crime rate.

25. The investigative function does not require any input from the regular patrol officer.

26. Sting operations have netted millions of dollars in recovered property and resulted in the arrest of numerous criminals.

27. Neighborhood policing is essential if police are to acquire an understanding of community problems.

28. Police productivity refers primarily to the number of arrests made by the police over a certain time period.

29. The time-in-rank promotion system enables quick promotion of qualified candidates.

30. Television programs and movies often present a distorted and romanticized view of policing.

31. Variations in patrol techniques appeared to have a major effect on citizens' attitudes toward police and their fear of future criminal activity.

32. Community and problem-oriented policing models stress social service over crime deterrence

33. An evaluation of foot patrol indicates that although crime rates did not decrease, residents in areas of increased foot patrols perceived greater safety.

34. Officers in one-person cars are just as safe and productive as officers in two-person cars.

35. A patrol officer's tour of duty typically includes several arrests.

36.   An increase in the arrest rate can help reduce an area's overall crime rate.

37.   Police officers may be reluctant to change their style of policing.

38.   Once a crime has been completed, the chances of identifying and arresting a suspect diminish rapidly.

39.   The amount and type of preservice training for police officers is relatively standard throughout police departments.

MULTIPLE CHOICE

40.   The time-in-rank method for determining promotion requires an officer to do which of the following.

        a.   have served at least 3 years on patrol
        b.   have spent time as a community service officer
        c.   spend his/her free time coaching sports
        d.   spend a certain amount of time in the next lowest rank

41.   Maintaining public order ("peacekeeping") is a major purpose of which of the following.

        a.   patrol
        b.   administration
        c.   investigation
        d.   internal affairs

42.   The Kansas City study indicated that variations in patrol techniques did which of the following.

        a.   had little effect on crime patterns
        b.   had little effect on citizen's attitude toward police
        c.   had little effect on citizens fear of crime
        d.   all of the above

43.   Rand researchers estimated that _____ of all detectives could be replaced without negatively affecting crime clearance rates.

        a.   15%
        b.   25%
        c.   50%
        d.   75%

Chapter 6

44. A _____ approach to policing is to respond when a citizen initiates a service call.

    a. proactive
    b. positive
    c. reactive
    d. both a and b

45. Which of the following is descriptive of discretion.

    a. unimportant to policing
    b. important and necessary to policing
    c. beyond control of the police
    d. none of the above

46. Which of the following practice(s) is/are used to increase police productivity.

    a. use of multiple-tasking
    b. use of civilian employees
    c. pooling of resources
    d. all of the above

47. Which of the following functions are **not** part of the police role.

    a. peacekeeping
    b. order maintenance
    c. investigation
    d. all of the above are functions of the police role

48. If a crime is reported while in progress, approximately what chance do police have of making an arrest:

    a. 20%
    b. 30%
    c. 40%
    d. 50%

49. A patrol officer averages approximately how many arrests per month.

    a. 1-2
    b. 3-5
    c. 7-9
    d. 10-12

50. To improve investigatory effectiveness PERF recommends greater emphasis be placed on:

    a. collection of physical evidence
    b. identifying witnesses
    c. using informants
    d. all of the above

51. Which of the following can result from undercover work.

    a. disrupted family relationships
    b. physical danger
    c. psychological problems
    d. all of the above are dangers of undercover work

52. An average of how many days elapses between a report and the suspension of an investigation.

    a. 7
    b. 11
    c. 13
    d. 21

53. Which of the following reflects the broken windows approach.

    a. neighborhood disorder creates fear
    b. neighborhoods give crime-promoting signals
    c. police need citizen cooperation
    d. all of the above are part of the broken windows approach

54. Approximately what percentage of police departments require preservice training.

    a. 10%
    b. 30%
    c. 60%
    d. 90%

55. Approximately what percentage of police departments disqualify candidates with misdemeanor convictions.

    a. 10%
    b. 50%
    c. 70%
    d. 100%

56. What percentage of departments employ polygraph exams for potential officers.

   a.   less than 10%
   b.   20%
   c.   30%
   d.   more than 50%

57. _____ involves setting aside areas where a special level of service is provided and financed through a special tax or assessment.

   a.   Creating police service districts
   b.   Pooling
   c.   Contracting
   d.   Consolidation

MATCHING

58.   Time-in-rank   A.   Responding only when summoned

59.   Proactive Patrol   B.   Prohibits rapid advancement

60.   Reactive Patrol   C.   Neighborhoods give out crime-promoting signals

61.   Broken Windows   D.   Aggressive law enforcement

62.   Problem-oriented policing (POP)   E.   Bottom-up decision making

63.   Decentralization   F.   Connectedness

64.   Community oriented policing (COP)   G.   "Hot spots" of crime

ESSAY QUESTIONS

65. Discuss the implications for policing suggested by the following studies: Kansas City study on preventive patrol; the study on detectives and investigation effectiveness; and the various studies on foot patrol and community policing.

66. Discuss how community oriented policing (COP) differs from other policing strategies, and what steps would need to be taken to implement such a program.

67. Should a police chief be permitted to promote an officer with special skills to a supervisory position, or should all officers be forced to spend "time-in-rank?" Explain.

68. What do you feel is the best measure of police productivity and why?

69. Discuss the major role or responsibility you feel the police should concentrate on in a democratic society.

CHAPTER SIX ANSWER SECTION

FILL-IN REVIEW

1.   Patrol officers, 60
2.   beat
3.   order, peacekeeping
4.   Kansas City, patrol
5.   proactive
6.   sting, detectives, illegal
7.   police-community
8.   broken windows
9.   community, problem-oriented
10. internal affairs
11. Police productivity
12. Multiple-tasking
13. Consolidation
14. selective enforcement
15. displacement
16. bottom-up
17. Formal, specific
18. Kansas City Gun, fifty
19. ten

SELF TEST

True/False

20.	T	30.	T
21.	F	31.	F
22.	T	32.	T
23.	T	33.	T
24.	F	34.	T
25.	F	35.	F
26.	T	36.	T
27.	T	37.	T
28.	F	38.	T
29.	F	39.	F

MULTIPLE CHOICE

40.	D	49.	A
41.	A	50.	D
42.	D	51.	D
43.	C	52.	B
44.	C	53.	D
45.	B	54.	D
46.	D	55.	B
47.	D	56.	D
48.	B	57.	A

MATCHING

58.	B
59.	D
60.	A
61.	C
62.	G
63.	E
64.	F

7   Issues in Policing

LEARNING OBJECTIVES

1. Explain what is meant by police culture and the core values associated with it.

2. Describe the origin and several aspects of the police personality.

3. List and discuss the four major police officer styles.

4. Discuss police discretion and the factors influencing it.

5. Describe the impact of higher education on police officers.

6. Identify the changing composition of police personnel.

7. Describe the unique difficulties confronting minority officers in police departments.

8. Describe the performance of female officers.

9. Discuss some of the factors associated with police stress and various coping techniques.

10. Differentiate between brutality and deadly force.

11. Define police corruption and several approaches that can be used to curb illegal police activities.

CHAPTER SUMMARY

Police experts have found that the experience of becoming a police officer and the nature of the job contribute to the development of a unique **police personality**, which includes traits such as authoritarianism, racism, conservatism, cynicism and insecurity. There are two opposing viewpoints on the cause of this phenomenon. One holds that the police profession attracts people who have these traits before their policing careers. The other position maintains that socialization and on the job experience cause these traits to develop. There is also some evidence which suggests that a **police culture**, stressing secrecy and insulation from others, develops around the police personality.

Research indicates that police officers develop a particular working attitude or **style**. Four such styles have been identified: the **crime fighter**, who stresses the investigation of serious crimes and the prosecution of criminals; the **social agent**, who believes police should be involved in problem-solving; the **law enforcer**, who tends to emphasize detection and apprehension; and the **watchman**, who emphasizes the maintenance of public order rather than law enforcement or general service activities.

Regardless of their personal style, police officers use a tremendous amount of **discretion** in carrying out their daily duties. There are several factors which influence police discretion. The work **environment**, including factors such as personal values and racial makeup of a city, influence discretion. **Departmental** factors such as policies, practices, and customs of the local police department influence discretion. **Situational** factors attached to a particular crime provide another important influence on police actions and behavior. Studies have found that officers rely heavily on **demeanor** (the attitude and appearance of the offender) in making decisions. **Extralegal** factors also have an influence on officer discretion; factors such as race, class, and gender can influence arrest decisions.

Higher education for the police has been recommended by national commissions on policing since 1931. Despite the growth of educational opportunities for police, the issue of requiring advanced education for the field is not a simple one. For example, the evidence is not clear on the benefits provided by a college degree or even the type of education preferred.

Other key issues in policing include the growing population of women and minority officers. Recent research indicates that women are becoming highly successful police officers. While the percentage of minorities on police forces generally reflects their representation in the population, the number of female officers still lags behind. There is, however, a slowing increasing number of women and minorities in supervisory positions. Discrimination is an issue police departments will have to address for many years to come.

Job related **stress** continues to be a problem in police departments. Police psychologists have divided stressors into four distinct categories. **External** stressors which include verbal abuse from the public, system inefficiency and liberal court decisions. **Organizational** stressors consist of things like low pay, excessive paperwork, arbitrary rules and limited opportunity for advancement. **Duty** stressors consist of rotating shifts, work overload, boredom, fear and danger. **Individual** stressors include discrimination, marital difficulties, and personality problems. Stress training combines information on diet, biofeedback, relaxation and meditation, and exercise for stress reduction.

Today, police **brutality**--from abusive language to the unnecessary use of force--and the use of **deadly force** in apprehending fleeing or violent offenders, are critical issues with respect to public safety. Both of these areas continue to be of concern to police administrators as they attempt to develop policies and procedures to eliminate and control abusive or illegal actions. In 1985, the U.S. Supreme Court outlawed the indiscriminate use of deadly force with its decision in the case of *Tennessee v. Garner*. Since their inception, U.S. police departments have wrestled with the problem of controlling **corruption**, the illegal and unprofessional behavior of police officers. There are several approaches that can be taken to control behavior with restrictive policies, but the greatest changes may come form the threat of civil litigation.

KEY TERMS AND CONCEPTS

Police Culture
Blue Curtain
Cynicism
Police Personality
Graham v. Connor
Crime Fighter
Social Agent
Law Enforcer
Watchman
Discretion
Demeanor
Double Marginality
U.S. v. Paradise
Civil Liability

Stress
Police Brutality
Deadly Force
Tennessee v. Garner
Christopher Commission
Deliberate Indifference
Knapp Commission
"Meat Eaters"
"Grass Eaters"
Mollen Commission
Rotten Pocket
Accountability System
Defeminization
Low visibility decision making

FILL-IN REVIEW

1.   Police experts have found that the experience of becoming a police officer and the nature of the job causes officers to band together in a police _____, characterized by clannishness, secrecy, and insulation from others in society. This is referred to as the

_____   _____.

2.   The policeman's "_____   _____" is shaped by constant exposure to danger and the need to use _____ and authority to reduce and control threatening situations.

Issues in Policing

3.   One of the most important findings of Niederhoffer's study of New York City officers, was that police _____ increased with _____ of service.

4.   The Crime Fighter can be distinguished from the Law Enforcer in that the latter does not separate between _____ and _____ crimes.

5.   The _____ _____ believes that police should get involved in a wide range of activities and assist special needs populations.

6.   The Watchman emphasizes the maintenance of public _____ as the primary police goal.

7.   During the course of their daily activities, police officers exercise a great deal of _____ .

8.   Nicholas Alex uses the term "_____ _____" in reference to the black officer's dilemma of expectations to give members of his own race a break, and overt racism from his police colleagues.

9.   The case of _____ v. _____ upheld racial quotas as a means of reversing past discrimination.

10. Minorities and women tend to be _____ in police departments.

11. In the Washington D.C. study of police women, it was found that women were more likely than their male colleagues to receive _____ from the community and were less likely to be charged with _____ conduct.

12. _____ is the process of labeling women who prove themselves tough enough so as to neutralize their threat to male dominance.

13. Discrimination, marital difficulties, and personality problems are _____ stressors.

14. Regarding police _____, the evidence suggests that actual instances of physical abuse of citizens by police is _____ frequent than commonly imagined.

15. The threat of _____ _____ may prove the most effective deterrent yet to control the police use of excessive force.

16. _____ _____ refers to the actions of a police officer who shoots and kills a suspect who is either fleeing from an arrest, assaulting a victim, or attacking the police officer.

17.   The case of _____ v. _____ outlawed the indiscriminate use of deadly force.

18.   The Knapp Commission classified corruption among police officers into two categories: "_____ eaters" and "_____ eaters."

SELF TEST

True/False

19.   Most evidence suggests that a police personality is developed through the on-going process of doing police work.

20.   Researchers have generally concluded that a unique police personality does not exist.

21.   Policing involves a multitude of diverse tasks other than crime-fighting.

22.   Scholars have concluded that most police officers use a high degree of personal discretion in carrying out daily tasks.

23.   There is clear-cut evidence that college educated police perform better on their daily activities than do non-educated officers.

24.   The racial and gender composition of a police department's supervisory staff should reflect the number of minorities and women on the department.

25.   *United States v. Paradise* denied racial quotas as a means of reversing the effects of past discrimination.

26.   The development of higher education for police officers has been recommended by national commissions on policing since 1931.

27.   College-educated officers tend to receive fewer citizen complaints.

28.   Studies show that women officers perform just as well with male or female officers as partners.

29.   Recent research indicates that female officers tend to have lower levels of performance than their male colleagues.

30.   Police experience a disproportionate number of premature deaths caused by coronary heart disease and diabetes.

31.   Early police officers often resorted to violence and intimidation to gain the respect of citizens.

32.   Research suggests that physical abuse of citizens by police officers is less frequent than commonly imagined.

33.   Every year less than thirty law enforcement and public safety officers are feloniously killed in the line of duty.

34.   Force is considered excessive when, considering all the circumstances known to the officer at the time he acted, the force was unreasonable.

35.   Police officers use formal arrest procedures more often in lower-class neighborhoods than middle or upper-class neighborhoods.

36.   The existence of available social agencies as an alternative to the criminal justice system often influences the decision regarding formal arrest procedures.

37.   The arrest rates for male officers are significantly higher than the arrest rates for female officers.

38.   The Christopher Commission concluded that the Los Angeles Police Department kills and/or wounds more citizens than any other big-city department.

MULTIPLE CHOICE

39.   The strategy of maintaining a low profile and intervening only when there is a clear indication of public danger is that of a:

    a.   Crime Fighter
    b.   Social Agent
    c.   Watchman
    d.   Law Enforcer

40.   The style of policing in which the officer considers himself to be a problem-solver is:

    a.   Watchman
    b.   Social Agent
    c.   Crime Fighter
    d.   Law Enforcer

Chapter 7

41. The style of police work in which the officer is interested primarily in dealing with "hard" crimes is called the:

    a. Social Agent
    b. Crime Fighter
    c. Law Enforcer
    d. Watchman

42. _____ is/are an example(s) of a situational influence on discretion exercised by police.

    a. Demeanor
    b. Manner in which a crime is encountered
    c. Personal matters
    d. all of the above

43. Race, gender, and economic status are _____ factors that can relate to police discretion.

    a. environmental
    b. situational
    c. extralegal
    d. departmental

44. Racial quotas with the intent of reversing past discrimination were upheld in the case of:

    a. *Tennessee v. Garner*
    b. *Lassiter v. Department of Social Services*
    c. *Graham v. Connor*
    d. *U.S. v. Paradise*

45. Today, about _____ percent of all sworn officers are women.

    a. 8
    b. 16
    c. 24
    d. 32

46. Which of the following is associated with enormous stress resulting in decreased police effectiveness.

    a. complexity of police role
    b. Internal Affairs division
    c. danger of police role
    d. both a and c

47. Which of the following is **not** an organizational stressor.

    a. workload
    b. low pay
    c. excessive paper work
    d. all of the above are organizational stressors

48. Which of the following is **not** considered police brutality.

    a. abusive language
    b. prodding with nightsticks
    c. threats
    d. all of the above are considered police brutality

49. Deadly force refers to the actions of a police officer who shoots and kills a suspect who is engaging in which of the following.

    a. fleeing from arrest
    b. assaulting a victim
    c. attacking the police officer
    d. all of the above

50. Which of the following factors does **not** relate to police shootings.

    a. firearm availability
    b. social variables
    c. police workload
    d. all of the above relate to police shootings

51. Which category of police corruption involves participation by police in serious criminal behaviors.

    a. bribery and extortion
    b. active criminality
    c. selective enforcement or nonenforcement
    d. none of the above

52. The _____ system holds that police departments at each level of command are accountable for the illegal behaviors of the officers under them.

    a. scrutiny
    b. authoritarian
    c. "tight"
    d. none of the above

53.   Fyfe attributes his finding that black officers were almost twice as likely as white officers to have shot citizens to the fact that.

      a.   black officers hold proportionately more line positions
      b.   black officers hold more administrative posts
      c.   black officers work and live in high-crime areas
      d.   both a and c

54.   Approximately what percentage of police departments require a two-year college degree.

      a.   8%
      b.   10%
      c.   20%
      d.   40%

55.   By 1950, what percentage of all police officers were minorities.

      a.   0%
      b.   2%
      c.   8%
      d.   12%

MATCHING

56.   *Behind the Shield*   A.   Accountability System

57.   *U.S. v. Paradise*   B.   Departmental Discrimination

58.   *Prince of the City*   C.   Double Marginality

59.   *Tennessee v. Garner*   D.   Police Corruption

60.   *Black in Blue*   E.   Police Personality

61.   *Canton v. Harris*   F.   Deadly Force

62.   Knapp Commission   G.   Deliberate Indifference

ESSAY QUESTIONS

63.   Describe four major styles of police work; which style do you think is the most appropriate for your community and why?

64.   Discuss the different factors which influence an officer's use of discretion.

65.   Give several reasons why a college degree should or should not be a requirement to become a police officer.

66.   Briefly discuss why police departments should attempt to hire qualified women and minority group members.

67.   Describe several methods departments can utilize to help reduce officer stress.

68.   Describe and defend a policy you think should be used regarding deadly force.

69.   Describe three of Sherman's categories of police corruption and several approaches that may be used to control corruption.

CHAPTER SEVEN ANSWER SECTION

FILL-IN REVIEW

1. subculture, blue curtain
2. working personality, force
3. cynicism, length
4. major, minor
5. Social Agent
6. order
7. discretion
8. double marginality
9. *U.S. v. Paradise*
10. under represented
11. support, improper
12. Defeminization
13. individual
14. brutality, less
15. civil litigation
16. Deadly force
17. *Tennessee v. Garner*
18. meat, grass

SELF TEST

True/False

19.	T	29.	F
20.	F	30.	T
21.	T	31.	T
22.	T	32.	T
23.	F	33.	F
24.	T	34.	T
25.	F	35.	T
26.	T	36.	T
27.	T	37.	F
28.	F	38.	T

MULTIPLE CHOICE

39.	C		48.	D
40.	B		49.	D
41.	B		50.	D
42.	D		51.	B
43.	C		52.	D
44.	D		53.	D
45.	A		54.	A
46.	D		55.	B
47.	A			

MATCHING

56.	E
57.	B
58.	D
59.	F
60.	C
61.	G
62.	A

8   Police and the Rule of Law

LEARNING OBJECTIVES

1.   List and describe the primary investigative functions performed by law enforcement officers.

2.   Explain the significance of the search and seizure requirements of the Fourth Amendment.

3.   Define the concepts of unreasonableness, probable cause, and particularity as related to search warrants.

4.   List the procedural requirements that must be met to obtain a warrant.

5.   Describe several major exceptions to the search warrant requirements of the Fourth Amendment and related court cases.

6.   Explain the significance of *Chimel v. California*, *Terry v. Ohio*, *United States v. Ross*, *Katz v. United States* and *Mapp v. Ohio*.

7.   List the conditions that must exist for an arrest.

8.   Describe the conditions under which an arrest can be made without a warrant.

9.   Identify the circumstances under which the *Miranda* warnings must be given.

10.   Discuss the rights of the accused during the pretrial identification process.

11.   Explain how recent cases illustrate a weakening of the protection granted by *Miranda*.

12.   Describe future prospects for the exclusionary rule.

CHAPTER SUMMARY

Criminal detection, apprehension and arrest are the primary investigative functions performed by law enforcement officers. The police use numerous techniques to investigate crime and collect the evidence needed for criminal prosecution. Statutes and constitutional law place limitations on police investigation methods such as search and seizure, warrantless searches, arrest, custodial interrogation and lineups.

Evidence collected by the police is governed by the **search and seizure** requirements of the Fourth Amendment. The police can undertake a proper search and seizure if a valid **search warrant** has been obtained from the court. To be valid, the warrant must meet the criteria of **probable cause** and **particularity**, and must not be considered **unreasonable**.

There are exceptions to the search warrant requirement of the Fourth Amendment including searches incident to a lawful arrest, field interrogation (stop-and-frisk procedures), consent searches, automobile searches bus sweeps, drug courier profiles and evidence in plain view. Supreme Court cases such as *Chimel v. California*, *Terry v. Ohio* and *United States v. Ross* have clarified the scope of these exceptions. Evidence which is obtained in violation of the Fourth Amendment can be excluded from use in a criminal prosecution; this is referred to as the **exclusionary rule**.

The police can initiate an arrest with or without an **arrest warrant** once probable cause has been established. An arrest may be made without a warrant only if the law of the given jurisdiction allows for warrantless arrests, and probable cause has been established. As a result of the landmark case of *Miranda v. Arizona*, suspects taken into custody must be warned of their Fifth Amendment rights against self-incrimination before they are questioned. Numerous issues surrounding the *Miranda* ruling continue to be litigated, and it appears that the Supreme Court has weakened the ruling in recent years. Legal issues related to lineups and other identification procedures have also been reviewed by the courts.

The future of the exclusionary rule is one of the most controversial issues in the criminal justice system. While the Supreme Court has limited its application in recent years, the exclusionary rule still generally prohibits the admission of evidence that violates the defendant's constitutional rights.

Chapter 8

KEY TERMS AND CONCEPTS

Exclusionary Rule
Search and Seizure
Fourth Amendment
Search Warrant
Unreasonableness
Probable Cause
Particularity
Warrantless Searches
Hearsay Evidence
Arrest Warrant
Stop-and-Frisk
Terry v. Ohio
California v. Greenwood
United States v. Ross
Kirby v. Illinois
Neil v. Biggers
Electronic Surveillance
Good Faith Exception
Florida v. Bostick
Delaware v. Prouse

Consent
Plain View
Open Fields
Curtilage
Arrest
Miranda v. Arizona
Escobedo v. Illinois
Inevitable Discovery Rule
Detain
Drug Courier Profiles
Arizona v. Evans
Katz v. United States
Minnesota v. Dickerson
Chimel v. California
Weeks v. United States
Wolf v. Colorado
Mapp v. Ohio
U.S. v. Leon
Illinois v. Gates
Maryland v. Wilson

FILL-IN REVIEW

1. The _____ _____ "punishes" police by excluding from trial any evidence obtained in violation of the suspect's constitutional rights.

2. Criminal _____, apprehension, and _____ are the primary investigative functions performed by law enforcement officers.

3. Evidence collected by the police is governed by _____ and _____ requirements of the _____ Amendment.

4. A _____ _____ is a court order authorizing and directing the police to search a designated place for _____ stated in the order.

5. _____ in searches and seizures generally refers to whether an officer exceeds the scope of police authority.

6. A search warrant cannot be issued unless _____ _____ is supported by oath or affirmation of a police officer.

Police and the Rule of Law

7. A search warrant must specify the place to be searched and the reasons for searching it; this is known as _____.

8. Evidence used by police which originates with a police _____ is normally referred to as _____ evidence.

9. With a limited _____ and _____ power, a police officer is able to investigate suspicious persons and situations without having to meet the _____ _____ standard for arrest.

10. The Supreme Court has continued to interpret the _____ v. _____ case as an exception to the general rule requiring probable cause for arrest.

11. Police have been given the right to _____ suspects with less than probable cause.

12. The _____ search of an automobile is valid if the police have probable cause to believe that the car contains _____ they are seeking.

13. Those who give their _____ to search essentially _____ their constitutional rights under the Fourth Amendment.

14. Police can search for and seize evidence without benefit of a _____ if it is in _____ _____.

15. The police must normally request a _____ _____ based on probable cause before using electronic _____ equipment.

16. An _____, the first formal police procedure in the criminal process, occurs when a police officer takes a person into custody or _____ a person of their _____ for having allegedly committed a criminal offense.

17. In the case of a felony, most jurisdictions provide that an officer may arrest a suspect without a warrant where probable cause exists even though the officer was not _____ when the offense was _____.

18. Regarding *Miranda*, a suspect who comes under police custody at the time of _____, must be warned of the right under the _____ Amendment to be free from _____ - _____ prior to any questioning.

19. The _____ _____ provides that all evidence obtained by illegal searches and seizures is inadmissible in criminal trials.

20. Evidence gained illegally in a search, which does not fall under the exclusionary rule because it would eventually be found in the same condition, is known as the _____ _____ rule.

21. The _____ doctrine is usually interpreted to mean that the government must obtain an order if it wishes to listen into conversations in which the parties have a _____ expectation of _____.

22. The United States Supreme Court case of _____ established a "_____ _____" test to determine probable cause for issuing a search warrant.

SELF TEST

True/False

23. Unreasonableness in searches and seizures refers to whether an officer has adequately obtained a search warrant.

24. The police are generally not reluctant to seek a search warrant due to the lenient evidentiary standards of the court.

25. The stop-and-frisk procedure is a court standard allowing exploratory searches; it has not been codified through legislation.

26. Threshold inquiry refers to plain view searches.

27. Essentially, the same basic rules are applied to the search of a car as they are to a search of a home.

28. The police have been granted the right to detain suspects with less than probable cause.

29. The burden rests on the state to show that consent to a search was voluntarily given.

30. In executing a search warrant authorizing the search of a persons home, the police officer must knock on the door and announce his or her presence before using force to obtain entry.

31. Most arrests are made without a warrant.

32. In *Riverside County v. McLaughlin*, the Court stated that the police may detain an individual no longer than 24 hours without a probable cause hearing.

33. The *Miranda* warning must be given anytime a suspect is to be questioned.

34. In recent years, the Supreme Court has weakened the *Miranda* ruling.

35. The Supreme Court declared in *Miranda* that the police have a duty to warn defendants of their rights.

36. The *Miranda* decision denies police officers the opportunity to ask a suspect general questions as a witness at the scene of an unsolved crime.

37. A defendant has the right to counsel during a line-up, whether or not he has been formally charged with a crime.

38. The exclusionary rule was based on judicial, not legislative, decision making.

39. If an arrest is found to be invalid, any warrantless search incident to the arrest would be considered legal, and evidence obtained from the search could be used at trial.

40. In *Katz v. United States*, the Supreme Court decided that there is no actual trespass in electronic eaves dropping, and no warrant is required.

41. According to the *Chimel* doctrine, police can search a suspect without a warrant after a lawful arrest in order to secure evidence or to protect themselves from danger.

42. The accused has the right to have counsel present at a postindictment lineup or identification procedure.

43. There are no exceptions to the exclusionary rule.

MULTIPLE CHOICE

44. Evidence from a police informer is normally referred to as which of the following.

    a. second-hand evidence
    b. testimonial evidence
    c. hearsay evidence
    d. sworn evidence

45. Which of the following is/are an exception(s) to the search warrant requirement of the Fourth Amendment.

    a. field interrogation
    b. consent searches
    c. automobile searches
    d. all of the above are exceptions

Chapter 8

46. The Supreme Court's ruling in _____ v. _____ changed the policy in regard to the scope of a search incident to arrest to the defendant and the immediate physical surroundings under the defendant's control.

   a. *Dunaway v. New York*
   b. *Katz v. United States*
   c. *Terry v. Ohio*
   d. *Chimel v. California*

47. Which of the following cases was utilized by the Supreme Court to create the stop and frisk exception to the search warrant requirement.

   a. *Terry v. Ohio*
   b. *Chimel v. California*
   c. *Aguilar v. Texas*
   d. *Dunaway v. New York*

48. The case of _____ v. _____ concluded that if probable cause exists to believe that an automobile contains criminal evidence, a warrantless search by police is permissible.

   a. *United States v. Ross*
   b. *Chimel v. California*
   c. *Terry v. Ohio*
   d. none of the above

49. The main legal issue in consent searches is whether the person:

   a. knew that he could refuse consent
   b. was acting suspiciously
   c. voluntarily consented
   d. was sane

50. In_____ v. _____, the U.S. Supreme Court upheld the police drug interdiction technique of boarding buses, questioning passengers, and searching their luggage without suspicion of illegal activity.

   a. *Dunaway v. New York*
   b. *Florida v. Bostick*
   c. *Florida v. Royer*
   d. *Terry v. Ohio*

Police and the Rule of Law

51. For all practical purposes, a person is under arrest when:

    a.   he is deprived of his freedom
    b.   a police officer stops him
    c.   he is questioned by the police
    d.   all of the above

52. In most jurisdictions, a warrantless arrest for a felony requires which of the following.
    a.   probable cause
    b.   the officer's presence at the time of the crime
    c.   both a and b
    d.   none of the above

53. An arrest may be made without a warrant only where:

    a.   the officer is able to show probable cause that a crime occurred, and the person being arrested committed it
    b.   the law of the jurisdiction allows for arrest without a warrant
    c.   both a and b
    d.   none of the above

54. Protection against unreasonable search and seizure is found in which amendment of the U.S. Constitution.

    a.   First Amendment
    b.   Fourth Amendment
    c.   Sixth Amendment
    d.   Eighth Amendment

55. Which of the following controls the investigatory activities of police officers.

    a.   the rule of law
    b.   constitutional criminal procedure
    c.   both a and b
    d.   neither a nor b

56. Under *Chimel v. California*, a search incident to arrest can include what area.

    a.   the area in plain view
    b.   the area in the immediate=control of the suspect
    c.   the area of the suspect's person
    d.   there is no limitation on the area searched

Chapter 8

57.   Which Supreme Court case established the plain touch corollary to the plain view doctrine.

      a.   *Minnesota v. Dickerson*
      b.   *Carroll v. United States*
      c.   *Terry v. Ohio*
      d.   *United States v. Ross*

58.   Which Supreme Court case established the criteria related to pretrial identifications.

      a.   *U.S. v. Leon*
      b.   *Kirby v. Illinois*
      c.   *U.S. v. Wade*
      d.   *Neil v. Biggers*

59.   Which Supreme Court case(s) established the right to counsel at a postindictment lineup.

      a.   *U.S. v. Wade*
      b.   *Kirby v. Illinois*
      c.   both a and b
      d.   neither a nor b

60.   Which Supreme Court case held the exclusionary rule applicable to the states.

      a.   *U.S. v. Leon*
      b.   *Mapp v. Ohio*
      c.   *Wolf v. Colorado*
      d.   *Weeks v. U.S.*

61.   Which Supreme Court case established the good faith exception to the exclusionary rule.

      a.   *Mapp v. Ohio*
      b.   *U.S. v. Leon*
      c.   *Wolf v. Colorado*
      d.   *Weeks v. U.S.*

MATCHING

62.	*Terry v. Ohio*	A.	Right to privacy not restricted to certain physical places
63.	*Katz v. United States*	B.	Permissible scope of a search incident to lawful arrest
64.	*Illinois v. Gates*	C.	Privilege against self-incrimination
65.	*Miranda v. Arizona*	D.	Totality of circumstances
66.	*Chimel v. California*	E.	Automobile searches
67.	*United Sates v. Ross*	F.	Stop and frisk exception

ESSAY QUESTIONS

1. Discuss several of the major exceptions to the search warrant requirement of the Fourth Amendment; be sure to include what constitutes legality for each situation and give at least one example of each.

2. Describe the facts, the decision, and the significance of *Chimel v. California*.

3. Should illegally seized evidence be excluded from trial even though it is conclusive proof of a person's criminal acts? Explain your reasoning.

4. Discuss where the law stands today regarding warrantless searches of automobiles; what is the significance of *United States v. Ross*?

5. What is the purpose of a threshold inquiry or stop and frisk procedure?

6. Discuss the factors leading up to the *Miranda* decision and under what circumstances the warnings must be given; give several reasons why you agree or disagree with this ruling.

7. Does the exclusionary rule effectively deter police misconduct? Explain.

CHAPTER EIGHT ANSWER SECTION

FILL-IN REVIEW

1. exclusionary rule
2. detection, arrest
3. search, seizure, Fourth
4. search warrant, property
5. Unreasonableness
6. probable cause
7. particularity
8. informer, hearsay
9. stop, frisk, probable cause
10. *Terry v. Ohio*
11. detain
12. warrantless, evidence
13. consent, waive
14. warrant, plain view
15. court order, eavesdropping
16. arrest, deprives, freedom
17. present, committed
18. arrest, Fifth, self-incrimination
19. exclusionary rule
20. inevitable discovery
21. Katz, reasonable, privacy
22. *Illinois v. Gates*, "totality of circumstances"

SELF TEST

True/False

23.	F	34.	T
24.	F	35.	T
25.	F	36.	F
26.	F	37.	F
27.	F	38.	T
28.	T	39.	F
29.	T	40.	F
30.	T	41.	T
31.	T	42.	T
32.	F	43.	F
33.	F		

MULTIPLE CHOICE

44.	C	53.	C
45.	D	54.	B
46.	D	55.	C
47.	A	56.	B
48.	A	57.	A
49.	C	58.	D
50.	B	59.	C
51.	A	60.	B
52.	A	61.	B

MATCHING

62.	G
63.	A
64.	D
65.	C
66.	B
67.	F

9   Courts and the Judiciary

LEARNING OBJECTIVES

1. Explain the federal government's three tiered hierarchy of court jurisdiction.

2. Explain the significance of landmark decisions of the U.S. Supreme Court.

3. Identify the problems associated with the recent increases in civil and criminal litigation.

4. Define the role of the judge.

5. Describe at least three methods of judicial selection.

6. Discuss the unusual features of the United States Supreme Court, including how they choose cases and the significance of a court decision.

7. Identify some possible alternatives to relieve the current caseload congestion courts are facing.

8. Describe how technology is affecting court management.

9. Detail the four court unification models.

10. Explain the meaning of the "reasonable competence" standard.

CHAPTER SUMMARY

The **court** is a complex social agency which is the scene of many important elements of criminal justice decision-making: detention, jury selection, trial, and sentencing, which is usually composed of three separate systems. The **courts of limited jurisdiction**, commonly called **lower courts**, are restricted in the types of cases they hear. These courts handle misdemeanors and include special courts such as juvenile, family, and probate. In contrast, the **courts of general jurisdiction** handle serious civil and criminal matters. The **appellate courts** review questions of law appealed from the trial courts.

The federal government has established a three-tiered hierarchy of court jurisdiction. The **Federal District Courts** are the trial courts of the federal system. Appeals from the district courts are heard in one of twelve federal appeals courts, sometimes referred to as **Federal Appellate Courts**. These federal appellate courts also enforce orders of federal administrative agencies. The **U.S. Supreme Court** is the nation's highest appellate body. Rulings of the Supreme Court become a precedent that must be honored by all lower courts.

The **judge** is the senior officer in a court of criminal law. Judges have a variety of duties including rulings on conduct, evidence, procedure, sentencing and jury instructions. Several methods are used to select state court judges including appointments by governors or legislatures, popular election and the three-part approach known as the **Missouri Plan**.

Computers are becoming an important aid in the administration and management of courts. Computerized information retrieval is being utilized in judicial and administrative decision making, information handling and monitoring, and planning in court administration.

One approach to improving court efficiency has been the **unification** of trial courts into a single administrative body. Four such models exist, including the **constellation model**, the **confederation model**, the **federation model** and the **union model**.

KEY TERMS AND CONCEPTS

Defendants
Assembly-Line Justice
Courts of Limited Jurisdiction
Lower Courts
Courts of General Jurisdiction
Trial *de novo*
Appeal
Appellate Courts
State Supreme Court
Federal District Courts
Federal Appellate Courts
U.S. Supreme Court
Landmark Decision
Martin v. Hunter's Lessee

Court Caseload
Judge
Missouri (Merit) Plan
Unification
Constellation Model
Plea Bargaining
Confederation Model
Federation Model
Court Room Work Group
Union Model
Gun Court
Drug Court
Craft of Justice
Writ of Certiorari

FILL-IN REVIEW

1.   A _____ _____ group is where prosecutors, defense attorneys, judge and other court personnel try to handle the situation/case with as little fuss as possible.

2.   Overloaded court dockets have given rise to charges of "assembly-line justice" in which a majority of defendants are induced to plead _____, jury trials are rare, and the _____ trial is a highly desired but unattainable concept.

3.   Courts of _____ jurisdiction handle the more serious _____ cases, while courts of _____ jurisdiction handle _____.

4.   _____ courts review the procedures of a case in order to determine whether an _____ was made by judicial authorities.

5.   Each state has at least one court of _____ _____, usually called the state _____ court, which reviews issues of law and fact appealed from the trial courts.

6.   _____ _____ courts review decisions by trial courts and administrative agencies before they reach the supreme court stage.

7.   The federal government has established a three-tiered hierarchy of court jurisdiction, which, in order of ascendancy, consists of _____ Courts, Courts of _____, and the _____ Court.

8.   The Federal Court of Appeal are also known as _____ courts; there are _____ in number.

9.   The Supreme Court is composed of _____ members appointed for life terms by the _____ with approval of _____.

10.   When the U.S. Supreme Court decides to hear a case, it grants a writ of _____.

11.   A _____ decision by the U.S. Supreme Court becomes a _____ which must be honored by all lower courts.

12.   The significant increase in both _____ and _____ litigation has forced state and local governments to allocate even greater _____ to the courts.

13.   A judicial selection method consisting of a three-part approach is known as the _____ Plan.

14.   The _____ of trial courts into a single administrative body has been one attempt at improving court efficiency.

15.   Article 3, section 1 of the U.S. constitution created _____ courts.

16.   _____ of nine U.S. Supreme Court justices must vote to hear a class.

17.   The _____ model for court unification consists of a loose association whereby trial courts operate within local rules and procedures.

18.   The court unification system which is fully consolidated and highly centralized is the _____ model.

SELF TEST

True/False

19.   If a defendant believes that the procedures used in the case were in violation of his or her constitutional rights, the outcome of their case may be appealed.

20.   Plea negotiations and other non-judicial alternatives such as diversion are far less in number than the formal trial process.

21.   There are approximately 13,000 courts of limited jurisdiction in the United States.

22.   Appellate courts try felony cases.

23.   Criminal appeals represent a large percentage of the total number of cases processed by the nation.

24. The number of criminal appeals has been rising rapidly.

25. Recently, both criminal and civil litigation has significantly increased.

26. Trial *de novo* means that, on appeal, an entirely new trial is granted.

27. The overwhelming majority of general jurisdiction courts hear only serious criminal matters.

28. The federal appellate courts enforce orders of federal administrative agencies.

29. The U.S. District Courts are the trial courts of the federal system and their jurisdiction may overlap that of state courts.

30. The nation's appellate courts are the ones most often accused of "assembly-line justice."

31. The U.S. Supreme Court's action is the final step in settling constitutional criminal disputes throughout the nation.

32. When the U.S. Supreme Court hands down a decision, its ruling becomes precedent and must be honored by all lower courts.

33. The U.S. Supreme Court has discretion over most cases, and may choose to hear only those it deems important, appropriate or worthy of its attention.

34. A majority of states use popular election as their method for judicial selection.

35. Over one-half of the states have intermediate appellate courts.

36. Specialty courts such as the Cook County, Illinois Drug Court, have proven effective in reducing the processing time of drug cases.

37. All judges are required to have law degrees.

38. The use of mediation is one of the key components of the restorative justice model.

39. Few states use judicial nominating committees.

40. Today, all states use some form of central administration.

41. The various court unification models have been shown to have a great deal of influence on court performance.

MULTIPLE CHOICE

42.   Courts of limited jurisdiction include:

     a.   probate courts
     b.   juvenile courts
     c.   family courts
     d.   all of the above

43.   About _____ of the courts of general jurisdiction also have the responsibility of reviewing cases on appeal from courts of limited jurisdiction.

     a.   one-fourth
     b.   one-half
     c.   two-thirds
     d.   three-fourths

44.   The appellate court can:

     a.   order a new trial
     b.   allow the defendant to go free
     c.   uphold the original verdict
     d.   all of the above

45.   There are _____ federal courts of appeal.

     a.   9
     b.   12
     c.   16
     d.   23

46.   Federal courts of appeal are empowered to:

     a.   analyze judicial interpretation of the law
     b.   retry cases
     c.   determine whether facts brought out in trial support conviction or dismissal
     d.   all of the above

47.   Today there are _____ federal District Courts.

     a.   53
     b.   72
     c.   94
     d.   120

Chapter 9

48. Which of the following courts is responsible for enforcing orders from federal administrative agencies.

    a.   Federal Appeals Court
    b.   Federal District Court
    c.   U.S. Supreme Court
    d.   court of claims

49. At which state court level are the majority of serious offenses tried.

    a.   limited jurisdiction
    b.   courts of special jurisdiction
    c.   courts of general jurisdiction
    d.   none of the above

50. This famous decision reaffirmed the legitimacy of the U.S. Supreme Court's jurisdiction over state court decisions involving federal constitutional law.

    a.   *In re Gault*
    b.   *Martin v. Hunter's Lessee*
    c.   *Marvin v. Marvin*
    d.   *Hunter v. Louisiana*

51. Which of the following are **not** considered to be part of the Missouri Plan to select judges.

    a.   nonpartisan elections of incumbent judges
    b.   judicial nominating committee
    c.   judicial appointment by an elected official
    d.   all of the above are included in the Missouri Plan

52. Which state uses a highly structured union court model.

    a.   Connecticut
    b.   Utah
    c.   Montana
    d.   Alabama

53. Which of the following are judicial alternatives.

    a.   hiring a retired judge
    b.   part-time judges
    c.   dispute resolution
    d.   all of the above are judicial alternatives

Courts and the Judiciary

54. Which of the following have contributed to the caseload overflow.

    a. complexity of the law
    b. increased civil litigation
    c. both a and b
    d. neither a nor b

55. In the nations largest counties it can take up to _____ to adudicate a murder case.

    a. 1 year
    b. 6 months
    c. 4 months
    d. 8 weeks

56. Juvenile courts have jurisdiction over which of the following.

    a. status offenders
    b. neglected children
    c. juvenile delinquents
    d. all of the above

57. How many states distinguish between criminal and civil high courts.

    a. 2
    b. 8
    c. 16
    d. 24

58. Which of the following are judicial duties.

    a. ruling on appropriateness of conduct
    b. settling questions of evidence and procedure
    c. charging a jury on points of law
    d. all of the above are judicial duties

Chapter 9

MATCHING

59. District Courts

60. General Jurisdiction Courts

61. Circuit Courts

62. Appellate Courts

63. Municipal Courts

A. Federal Appeals Court

B. Misdemeanor Courts

C. Trial courts of federal system

D. Felony courts

E. Courts of last resort

ESSAY QUESTIONS

64. Briefly describe the functions of the three levels in the federal court hierarchy.

65. What does the term "assembly-line justice" mean; what can be done about it?

66. Discuss what is meant by a "landmark decision;" why are such decisions important?

67. Discuss what you consider to be the best method of judicial selection.

68. How can technology improve court management?

CHAPTER NINE ANSWER SECTION

FILL-IN REVIEW

1. Courtroom work
2. guilty, speedy
3. general, felony, limited, misdemeanors
4. Appellate, error
5. last resort, supreme
6. Intermediate appellate
7. District, Appeals, Supreme
8. circuit, twelve
9. nine, President, Congress
10. certiorari
11. landmark, precedent
12. civil, criminal, resources
13. Missouri
14. unification
15. federal
16. Four
17. Constellation
18. union

SELF TEST

True/False

19.	T	30.	F
20.	F	31.	T
21.	T	32.	T
22.	F	33.	T
23.	F	34.	T
24.	F	35.	T
25.	T	36.	T
26.	T	37.	F
27.	F	38.	T
28.	T	39.	F
29.	T	40.	T
		41.	F

MULTIPLE CHOICE

42.	D	51.	D
43.	D	52.	A
44.	D	53.	D
45.	B	54.	C
46.	A	55.	A
47.	C	56.	D
48.	A	57.	A
49.	C	58.	D
50.	B		

MATCHING

59.	C
60.	D
61.	A
62.	E
63.	B

10   The Prosecution and the Defense

LEARNING OBJECTIVES

1.   Define the role of the prosecutor; differentiate between federal and state/county prosecutors.

2.   Discuss prosecutorial misconduct and the possible repercussions associated with it.

3.   Define prosecutorial discretion and list several factors which may influence it.

4.   Discuss common factors which influence dismissals.

5.   Discuss several major U.S. Supreme Court decisions related to prosecutorial vindictiveness including *Blackledge v. Perry*, *Bordenkircher v. Hayes* and *U.S. v. Goodwin*.

6.   Explain the role of the criminal defense attorney and related ethical issues.

7.   Discuss the 6th Amendment right to counsel and the U.S. Supreme Court's interpretation of it.

8.   List the types of indigent defender systems in existence and describe the problems inherent in each program.

9.   Differentiate between the *ad hoc* assigned counsel system and the coordinated assigned counsel system.

10.   Discuss the significance of the U.S. Supreme Court case of *Strickland v. Washington*.

11.   Differentiate between the Frye test and the Daubert test and discuss how each affects evidence admissibility.

CHAPTER SUMMARY

The **prosecutor** is the state representative in criminal matters and may be known as a **district attorney, county attorney, state's attorney** or **U.S. attorney**. The prosecutor is generally a member of the practicing bar, appointed or elected to the position. The primary duty of the prosecutor is the enforcement of criminal law.

Prosecutorial misconduct is unethical behavior motivated by the desire to obtain a conviction. Appellate courts use the **harmless error doctrine** and generally uphold convictions where the misconduct is not considered serious. Prosecutors are not personally liable for such misconduct.

The prosecutor exercises a great deal of **discretion** in deciding whether or not to institute criminal proceedings, in selecting alternative dispositions, and in determining formal charges. Factors which influence these prosecutorial decisions include: available alternatives, cost of prosecution, attitude of victim, cooperativeness of suspect and the relationship between the defendant and victim. Several major U.S. Supreme Court cases have upheld the broad discretionary powers of prosecutors.

The **defense attorney** represents the accused in the criminal process. The accused may obtain private counsel, or, if indigent, private counsel or a **public defender** may be assigned by the court. The U.S. Supreme Court has judicially interpreted the **Fourth** and **Sixth Amendments** together to mean that counsel must be provided by the state to indigent defendants in all types of criminal proceedings. The Supreme Court has moved to extend the right to counsel to postconviction and other collateral proceedings. The Supreme Court has also established a **reasonable competence standard** for defense attorneys.

Public defender offices, organized at the state or county level, utilize public employees to provide legal services to indigent defendants. In contrast, the **assigned counsel system** involves the use of private attorneys appointed by the court. A third program, the **contract system**, provides a block grant or fixed fee to a lawyer or law firm to handle indigent defense cases. In some areas, **mixed systems** exist, utilizing both public defenders and private attorneys.

The admissibility of scientific evidence involves both prosecutors and defense attorneys. The **Frye test**, which is still used in most states holds that evidence is admissible if the methodology used is generally accepted in the scientific community. In 1993, the federal courts and some state courts adopted the **Daubert test** which allows expert testimony concerning scientific or technical knowledge that assists the trier of fact in understanding evidence presented.

KEY TERMS AND CONCEPTS

Prosecutor
District Attorney
U.S. Attorney
Attorney General
Town of Newton v. Rumery
United States v. Goodwin
Defense Attorney
Public Defender
Adversarial Process
Indigent Defendant
Sixth Amendment
Nolle Prosequi
Prosecutorial Vindictiveness
Pro Bono
Pretrial Diversion
Discretion
Conflict of Interest

Gideon v. Wainwright
Argersinger v. Hamlin
Contract System
Mixed Counsel System
Ad Hoc Assigned Counsel System
Coordinated Assigned Counsel System
Plea Bargaining
Burger v. Kemp
Taylor v. Illinois
Surprise Witness Rule
Reasonable Competence Standard
Strickland v. Washington
Frye Test
Daubert Test
Recoupment
Immunity
DNA testing

FILL-IN REVIEW

1. The key to the prosecutorial function is the power to institute formal _____ against the _____.

2. The process whereby the prosecutor drops charges after deciding not to pursue criminal proceedings is called _____ _____.

3. The prosecutor is an _____, public _____ and _____ of the court.

4. Too much prosecutorial _____ can lead to abuses which result in the abandonment of the law.

5. Prosecutors are political figures with party affiliations and are normally _____ or _____ to the office.

6. Many prosecutor's offices now have special _____ units which deal with crimes such as improper waste disposal.

7. The federal prosecutor is called a _____ _____ _____ and is appointed by the _____.

8. State prosecutors are called _____ _____ while county prosecutors are referred to as _____ _____.

9. _____ _____ is the postponement or elimination of prosecution in exchange for participation in a program such as drug rehabilitation.

10. According to the U.S. Supreme Court case of _____ v. _____ _____, no realistic likelihood of prosecutorial vindictiveness exists where a prosecutor increases charges after plea negotiations fail and the defendant requests a jury trial.

11. The court may assign an _____ defendant either private counsel or a _____ defender.

12. The U.S. Supreme Court case of _____ v. _____ established that counsel must be provided to indigent defendants in all criminal cases where the penalty can include imprisonment.

13. For many years the role of the criminal _____ attorney and the practice of criminal _____ have generally been afforded low status by the legal profession.

14. Programs providing the assistance of counsel to indigents are organized into three major categories: _____ defender systems, _____ counsel systems and _____ systems.

15. The _____ _____ system involves the use of private attorneys appointed by the _____ to represent indigent defendants.

16. An _____ _____ _____ counsel system is where a judge appoints attorneys to indigent defendants on a case-by-case basis.

17. In the _____ system, a block grant is given to a lawyer or law firm to handle _____ defense cases.

18. _____ systems use both public _____ and _____ attorneys to handle indigent defense cases.

19. Free legal aid to indigents is referred to as _____ _____ work.

20. _____ v. _____ dealt with the surprise witness rule.

21. There is a _____ _____ standard for defense attorneys.

SELF TEST

True/False

22. The American Bar Association's Code of Professional Responsibility deals with the ethical duties of an attorney as a prosecutor.

23. Federal prosecutors are known as United States attorneys and are elected to office.

24. There has been an increase in the local prosecution of corporate offenders and white-collar criminals.

25. Prosecutorial handling of rape cases has changed little in the last decade.

26. In felony cases, the prosecutor has little discretion in deciding whether to charge the accused with a crime.

27. The judge is the chief law enforcement officer of a specific jurisdiction.

28. The most common reason for case dismissal is insufficient evidence.

29. Conviction rates for cases involving strangers is higher than that for cases involving friends and/or relatives.

30. According to *Bordenkircher v. Hayes*, the U.S. Supreme Court will allow a prosecutor to carry out threats of increased charges where a defendant pleads not guilty.

31. Over 4.5 million offenders are given free legal services yearly.

32. Ethical rules may differ for prosecutors and defense attorneys.

33. There is no right to counsel at juvenile delinquency hearings, mental health commitments or parole revocation hearings.

34. There is a right to counsel at grand jury investigation.

35. Most jurisdictions utilize assigned counsel systems.

36. Much of the total justice system spending is for indigent defendant systems.

37. The majority of defendants are eventually brought to trial.

Chapter 10

38. Plea bargaining predominates because little time and insufficient resources are available to give criminal defendants a full-scale defense.

39. The concept of attorney competence was defined by the U.S. Supreme Court in the case of *Gideon v. Wainwright*.

40. Federal courts utilize the Frye test with regard to scientific evidence admissibility.

41. DNA evidence is more likely to be utilized under the Daubert test.

MULTIPLE CHOICE

42. In the criminal trial process, who has the authority to bring the accused to trial.

    a. police
    b. prosecutor
    c. judge
    d. all of the above

43. Which of the following activities are part of the prosecutor's role.

    a. tries criminal cases
    b. subpoenas witnesses
    c. determines formal charges
    d. all of the above

44. Prosecutorial discretion is beneficial for which of the following reasons.

    a. it ensures justice
    b. it allows for alternatives to criminal sanctions
    c. it serves as a screening process for cases
    d. both b and c

45. Which of the following is **not** a function of the defense counsel.

    a. providing assistance at sentencing
    b. investigating incidents
    c. providing assistance during grand jury investigation
    d. entering into plea negotiations

46.   Which of the following has **not** been identified as a factor influencing the prosecutor's charging decision.

      a.   the cost of prosecution
      b.   the suspects attitude toward the victim
      c.   the willingness of the suspect to cooperate
      d.   the available alternatives

47.   What is the average overall percentage conviction rate of state prosecutors.

      a.   45%
      b.   65%
      c.   85%
      d.   95%

48.   Which of the following are **non-traditional** prosecution efforts.

      a.   crimes against persons
      b.   computer fraud
      c.   plea bargaining negotiations
      d.   both b and c

49.   The National District Attorney's Association performs which of the following functions.

      a.   sets guidelines for plea bargains
      b.   assists in prosecution of environmental crimes
      c.   runs a national criminal database
      d.   none of the above

50.   Which of the following have been among changes in the handling of rape cases.

      a.   the definition of rape has been expanded
      b.   marital rape has been recognized
      c.   restrictions on the victim's sexual history
      d.   all of the above

51.   Which U.S. Supreme Court case did **not** relate to prosecutorial vindictiveness.

      a.   *Blackledge v. Perry*
      b.   *U.S. v. Goodwin*
      c.   *Burns v. Reed*
      d.   *Bordenkircher v. Hayes*

Chapter 10

52. At which of the following stages in the criminal process in there a right to counsel.

    a.   postindictment lineups
    b.   preindictment lineups
    c.   grand jury investigations
    d.   second appeals

53. Which of the following are reasons for underfunded counsel services for indigent criminal defendants.

    a.   caseload problems
    b.   lack of available attorneys
    c.   legislative restraints
    d.   all of the above

54. Which U.S. Supreme Court case dealt with the surprise witness rule.

    a.   *Burger v. Kemp*
    b.   *Taylor v. Illinois*
    c.   *Strickland v. Washington*
    d.   *North Carolina v. Pearce*

55. Which standard on admissibility of evidence do most states use.

    a.   Daubert test
    b.   Frye test
    c.   Strickland test
    d.   Washington test

56. Which U.S. Supreme Court case dealt with attorney competence.

    a.   *Argersinger v. Hamlin*
    b.   *U.S. v. Goodwin*
    c.   *Bordenkircher v. Hayes*
    d.   *Strickland v. Washington*

MATCHING

57.	*Gideon v. Wainwright*	A.	Prosecutorial vindictiveness
58.	*Argersinger v. Hamlin*	B.	Prosecutorial discretion
59.	*Blackledge v. Perry*	C.	Right to counsel where possible imprisonment
60.	*Town of Newton v. Rumery*	D.	Surprise Witness Rule
61.	*Taylor v. Illinois*	E.	Attorney Competence
62.	*Strickland v. Washington*	F.	Right to counsel for felony

ESSAY QUESTIONS

63. List several factors a prosecutor may properly consider in exercising a decision to charge a suspect.

64. Why was the role of the criminal defense attorney generally afforded low status? What recent changes have occurred?

65. Describe the three major systems which provide indigent defendants the assistance of counsel; identify the problems inherent in each.

66. Discuss the major U.S. Supreme Court cases related to prosecutorial discretion, vindictiveness and immunity.

67. Describe the conflicting obligations defense attorneys face.

68. Detail the historical development of the right to counsel.

69. Distinguish between the Frye test and the Daubert test. Which do you think is best? Explain.

CHAPTER TEN ANSWER SECTION

FILL-IN REVIEW

1.   charges, defendant
2.   *nolle prosequi*
3.   attorney, servant, officer
4.   discretion
5.   elected, appointed
6.   environmental
7.   United States attorney, President
8.   attorney generals, district attorneys
9.   Pretrial diversion
10. *U.S. v. Goodwin*
11. indigent, public
12. *Argersinger v. Hamlin*
13. defense, law
14. public, assigned, contract
15. assigned counsel court
16. *ad hoc* assigned
17. contract, indigent
18. Mixed, defenders, private
19. pro bono
20. *Taylor v. Illinois*
21. reasonable competence

SELF TEST

True/False

22.	T		32.	T
23.	F		33.	F
24.	T		34.	F
25.	F		35.	T
26.	F		36.	F
27.	F		37.	F
28.	T		38.	T
29.	T		39.	F
30.	T		40.	F
31.	T		41.	T

MULTIPLE CHOICE

42.	B	50.	D
43.	D	51.	C
44.	D	52.	A
45.	C	53.	D
46.	B	54.	B
47.	C	55.	B
48.	B	56.	D
49.	B		

MATCHING

57.	F
58.	C
59.	A
60.	B
61.	D
62.	E

11   Pretrial Procedures

LEARNING OBJECTIVES

1.   Explain how a criminal complaint is initiated.

2.   Differentiate between an indictment and an information.

3.   Describe the bail system.

4.   Discuss the success of bail and several reforms that are being tried.

5.   Differentiate between preventive detention and pretrial detention.

6.   Explain the operating differences between a grand jury and a preliminary hearing.

7.   Differentiate between a plea of guilty and *nolo contendere*.

8.   List several advantages and disadvantages of plea bargaining to the defendant and to the administration of justice system.

9.   Describe several reforms that are being used regarding plea bargaining.

10.   Explain how pretrial diversion programs work and the meaning of the term, "widening the net."

CHAPTER SUMMARY

After arrest, the accused is ordinarily taken to the police station, where the police list the possible criminal charges against the accused and obtain other information for **booking** purposes. In misdemeanor cases, the **complaint** is the formal written document identifying the criminal charge, the date and place of the crime, and the circumstances of the arrest. Where a felony is involved, the formal charging process is ordinarily an **indictment** from a **grand jury**, or an **information** through a **preliminary hearing**. The accused is then brought before the trial court for **arraignment**, during which the judge informs the defendant of the charge, ensures that the accused is properly represented by counsel, and determines whether the person should be released on bail or some other form of release pending a hearing or trial.

The use of money **bail** and other alternatives, such as **release on recognizance** (ROR), allow most defendants to be free pending their return for trial. Today, **preventive detention** statutes are being used to detain people who are considered a threat to themselves or the community. Since the Eighth Amendment to the U.S. Constitution guarantees that bail should be made available to almost all those accused of crime, the use of any form of pretrial detention is viewed by many as unconstitutional and unnecessary.

One of the most common practices in the criminal justice system is the process of **plea bargaining**, or the exchange of legal concessions by the state for a plea of guilty by the defendant. More than 90 percent of criminal convictions result from negotiated pleas of guilty. Because of overcrowded criminal court caseloads and the needs of the prosecution and defense, plea bargaining has become an essential, yet controversial part of the administration of justice. Proponents contend that it actually benefits both the state and the defendant by trimming costs as well as time, and the defendant may receive a reduced sentence. Opponents, on the other hand, argue that plea bargaining is objectionable because it encourages a defendant to waive the constitutional right to trial. There appears to be no ideal system of adjudication and disposition in the criminal justice process. Guidelines and safeguards, have been developed to make the process more visible and uniform.

Another important feature in the early court process is the placing of offenders into noncriminal **diversion** programs prior to their formal trial or conviction. Diversion involves suspension of formal criminal proceedings against an accused while that person participates in a community treatment program under court supervision. These programs vary in size but generally possess the same goal of constructively bypassing criminal prosecution by providing a reasonable alternative in the form of treatment, counseling or employment. Diversion programs have come under fire for their alleged failures, the most prominent criticism being that they **widen the net** of the justice system. This means that people put in diversion programs are the ones most likely to have been dismissed, so rather than limit their involvement with the system, diversion programs may actually increase it.

Chapter 11

KEY TERMS AND CONCEPTS

Pretrial Procedures
Booking
Complaint
Initial Hearing
Boykin v. Alabama
Santobello v. New York
Indictment
Information
Grand Jury
Preliminary Hearing
Probable Cause Hearing
Nolo contendere
Bail
Stack v. Boyle
Bail Bonding
Deposit Bail
Release on Recognizance (ROR)
Manhattan Bail Project
Bail Reform Act of 1966 and 1984
Hill v. Lockhart

Preventive Detention
Schall v. Martin
United States v. Salerno
Pretrial Detention
Presentment
Subpoena
Eighth Amendment
True Bill
No Bill
Waiver
Arraignment
Plea bargaining
Brady v. United States
Bordenkircher v. Hayes
Diversion
Widen the Net
Continuance
North Carolina v. Alford
U.S. v. Mezzanatto

FILL-IN REVIEW

1.   After arrest, the _____ is taken to the police station, where the police list the possible criminal charges and obtain other information for _____ purposes.

2.   The _____ is the formal written document identifying the criminal _____, the date and place of the crime, and the circumstances of the arrest.

3.   An _____ is a written accusation submitted to the _____ _____ by the prosecutor charging a person with a crime.

4.   An _____ is a charging document that uses a _____ _____ or a probable cause hearing to test its sufficiency.

5.   _____ _____ are those programs that screen arrestees and provide the bail setting magistrate concise summaries of an arrestees' personal background.

Pretrial Procedures

6. _____ represents money or some other security provided to the _____ to insure the appearance of the defendant.

7. With few exceptions, all persons are entitled to bail that is not _____, as stated by the _____ Amendment of the U.S. Constitution.

8. The right to pretrial freedom has been enunciated in the case of _____ v _____.

9. Release on _____ was pioneered by the Vera Institute of Justice in an experiment entitled the _____ _____ Project.

10. The _____ _____ Act of 1984 mandates that no one be kept in pretrial detention solely because they cannot afford the money bail.

11. _____ _____ statutes specify certain dangerous offenders be kept in confinement prior to _____ in order to protect themselves and/or the community.

12. The criminal defendant who is not eligible for bail or ROR is subject to _____ _____ in the local jail.

13. The concept of the grand jury was incorporated into the _____ Amendment of the U.S. Constitution.

14. The grand jury's function are two-fold: _____ and _____.

15. If the grand jury fails to find probable cause, a _____ bill is passed; if probable cause exists, a _____ bill is passed.

16. A unique aspect of the preliminary hearing is that the defendant has the alternative to _____ the proceeding.

17. An _____ takes place after an indictment or _____ is filed following a grand jury or _____ _____.

18. A plea of _____ _____, which is essentially a guilty plea, may only be entered at the discretion of the _____ and prosecutor.

19. _____ _____ has been defined as the exchange of legal concessions by the state for a plea of _____ by the defendant.

20. While punishment is more certain with plea bargains, it is more _____ with trials.

Chapter 11

SELF TEST

True/False

21. Regarding pretrial services, the general criteria to assess eligibility for release centers around whether or not the defendant has enough money to pay for bail.

22. If the defendant is released on bail but fails to appear in court at the stipulated time, the bail deposit is forfeited.

23. Many believe that money bail is a discriminatory pretrial procedure.

24. Research indicates that there is a strong relationship between the amount of bail and a person's race, age, economic status, and other social variables.

25. Failure rates for those released on bail are similar for state and federal jurisdictions.

26. ROR allows for the release of a defendant without any requirement of money bail.

27. More than 50 percent of those held in local jails have been accused of crimes, but not yet convicted.

28. Nationwide between 1982 and 1990, local jails have had over a 90 percent occupancy increase.

29. Evidence suggests that, if convicted, people who do not receive bail are much more likely to be sent to prison and to do more time than people who avoid pretrial detention.

30. The grand jury usually meets at the request of the judge; moreover, hearings are closed and secret.

31. An arraignment occurs subsequent to a grand jury or preliminary hearing.

32. Several constitutional rights are surrendered when an individual pleads guilty to a crime in court.

33. The highest probability of the acceptance of a plea bargain is where caseload pressures are greatest.

34. The court has the discretion to reject an inappropriately offered plea.

35. The Federal Rules of Criminal Procedure prohibit federal judges from participating in a plea bargain.

36.   The predominant criticism of diversion programs is that they "widen the net" of the justice system.

37.   Today, most diversion programs are supported by federal funds.

38.   The Eighth Amendment requires that all defendants receive bail.

39.   The sole purpose of bail is to ensure the defendant returns for future proceedings.

40.   Bonding agents have been abolished in some states and replaced by the state with the 10 percent cash-match system.

41.   The Manhattan Bail Project determined that the court could not make a reasonably good judgment regarding a defendant's return from release on recognizance with any amount of information.

42.   According to *North Carolina v. Alford* a defendant cannot plead guilty without admitting guilt.

43.   The American Bar Association supports judicial involvement in plea bargaining.

44.   The U.S. Supreme Court case of *U.S. v. Mezzanatto* allows for prosecutors to require, as part of plea negotiation, a defendant to agree that statements made during negotiations may be used for impeachment purposes during trial.

MULTIPLE CHOICE

45.   Pretrial services accomplish which of the following.

     a.   sentence arrestees to jail
     b.   read the individual his or her rights
     c.   work out a plea bargain
     d.   none of the above

46.   The right to pretrial freedom has been enunciated in which case.

     a.   *Brady v. United States*
     b.   *Stack v. Boyle*
     c.   *Bordenkircher v. Hayes*
     d.   *Santobello v. New York*

Chapter 11

47. Research indicates that failure rates for bail at the state and federal levels is:

    a. similar for both jurisdictions
    b. higher at the federal level
    c. higher at the state level
    d. rates fluctuate between both jurisdictions

48. With few exceptions, other than perhaps murder, all accused persons are entitled to bail that is not excessive, as stated in the _____ Amendment.

    a. Fourth
    b. Fifth
    c. Sixth
    d. Eighth

49. In _____ v. _____, the U.S. Supreme Court upheld the application of preventive detention statutes to juvenile offenders on the grounds that such detention is useful to protect the welfare of the minor and society as a whole.

    a. *Schall v. Martin*
    b. *Brady v. United States*
    c. *Betts v. New York*
    d. *Boykin v. Alabama*

50. The concept of the grand jury is incorporated into the _____ Amendment of the U.S. Constitution.

    a. Fourth
    b. Fifth
    c. Sixth
    d. Eighth

51. A report from the grand jury containing information about its investigations and often a recommendation of indictment is known as:

    a. *stare decisis*
    b. *nolo contendere*
    c. presentment
    d. true bill

Pretrial Procedures

52. When a grand jury fails to find probable cause, a _____ is passed.

    a.   true bill
    b.   presentment
    c.   no contest
    d.   no bill

53. The purpose of _____ is to require the prosecutor to present facts for the judge to determine if the defendant should be held over for trial.

    a.   preliminary hearing
    b.   indictment
    c.   plea bargaining
    d.   none of the above

54. When the defendant stands mute before the bench during an arraignment, a plea of _____ is entered.

    a.   *nolo contendere*
    b.   guilty
    c.   not guilty
    d.   guilty with explanation

55. More than _____ of the defendants appearing before the court plead guilty prior to the trial state.

    a.   20%
    b.   40%
    c.   75%
    d.   90%

56. In which of the following court cases did the Supreme Court hold that the breaking of a plea bargain agreement, by the prosecutor, would result in reversal for the defendant.

    a.   *Brady v. United States*
    b.   *Santobello v. New York*
    c.   *Betts v. New York*
    d.   *Boykin v. Alabama*

57. It is the responsibility of the _____ to see that the accused understands the nature of the plea bargaining process and the guilty plea.

    a.   judge
    b.   prosecutor
    c.   defense attorney
    d.   both a and c

Chapter 11

58. Plea bargaining can consist of which of the following.

    a.   reduction of charges for guilty plea
    b.   reduction of number of counts for guilty plea
    c.   recommendation of lenient sentence for guilty plea
    d.   plea bargaining can consist of all of the above.

59. At the arraignment, the defendant:

    a.   is informed of charges
    b.   is informed of right to remain silent
    c.   enters a plea
    d.   both a and c

60. According to the Bail Reform Act of 1984, pretrial detention is acceptable when:

    a.   the defendant cannot pay money bail
    b.   nothing else will assure defendant's return
    c.   the defendant has a prior criminal record
    d.   the defendant has a bad attitude.

61. Diversion programs benefit defendants in which of the following ways.

    a.   allowing them to avoid criminal stigma
    b.   providing them rehabilitation
    c.   reducing their court costs
    d.   allowing them to escape punishment

62. In *Brady v. U.S.* the U.S. Supreme Court determined that a guilty plea was
    _____ if entered into solely to avoid the death penalty.

    a.   invalid
    b.   valid
    c.   valid only in certain cases
    d.   none of the above

63. Before a judge accepts a guilty plea, there must be an affirmative action indicating that the plea was:

    a.   reasonable
    b.   necessary
    c.   voluntary
    d.   coerced

MATCHING

64.	Indictment	A.	Money or some other security provided to court to insure the appearance of defendant
65.	Information	B.	Exchange of legal concessions by the state for a plea of guilty by the defendant
66.	Bail	C.	Charging document used in a preliminary hearing
67.	Arraignment	D.	Court appearance at which the judge informs the defendant of the charges against him
68.	Plea Bargaining	E.	Written accusation drawn up and submitted to the grand jury by the prosecutor

ESSAY QUESTIONS

69. What is the bail system and why is it considered to be unsatisfactory? Describe several recent reforms.

70. What are the legal consequences of a defendant's plea of guilty? What precautions must a judge take because of these?

71. Plea bargaining is a widespread aspect of the criminal justice system; what are the major advantages and disadvantages of this process?

72. Discuss the major advantages and disadvantages of the grand jury and preliminary hearing systems.

73. Should a judge participate in plea bargaining? Explain.

74. Define the concept of preventive detention and explain why you feel it should or should not be allowed.

75. Are pretrial diversion programs primarily beneficial for defendants? Explain why or why not.

CHAPTER ELEVENT ANSWER SECTION

FILL-IN REVIEW

1. accused, booking
2. complaint, charge
3. indictment, grand jury
4. information, preliminary hearing
5. Pretrial services
6. Bail, court
7. excessive, Eighth
8. *Stack v. Boyle*
9. recognizance, Manhattan Bail
10. Bail Reform
11. Preventive detention, trial
12. pretrial detention
13. Fifth
14. investigatory, accusatory
15. no, true
16. waive
17. arraignment, information, preliminary hearing
18. *nolo contendere*, judge
19. Plea bargaining, guilty
20. severe

SELF TEST

True/False

21.	F	33.	F
22.	T	34.	T
23.	T	35.	T
24.	F	36.	T
25.	F	37.	F
26.	T	38.	F
27.	T	39.	T
28.	T	40.	T
29.	T	41.	F
30.	F	42.	F
31.	T	43.	F
32.	T	44.	T

MULTIPLE CHOICE

45.	D		55.	D
46.	B		56.	B
47.	C		57.	C
48.	D		58.	D
49.	A		59.	D
50.	B		60.	B
51.	C		61.	A
52.	D		62.	B
53.	A		63.	C
54.	C			

MATCHING

64.	E
65.	C
66.	A
67.	D
68.	B

12   The Criminal Trial

LEARNING OBJECTIVES

1. Define the confrontation clause of the Sixth Amendment and recent U.S. Supreme Court case law on the subject.

2. Describe the defendant's right to a jury trial using U.S. Supreme Court case law.

3. Discuss the U.S. Supreme Court cases of *Williams v. Florida* and *Apodica v. Oregon* as they relate to jury size and unanimity.

4. Discuss the landmark U.S. Supreme Court cases related to a defendant's right to counsel at trial.

5. Explain the defendant's right to proceed *pro se.*

6. List the four purposes for the right to a speedy trial as highlighted in *Klopfer v. North Carolina.*

7. List the time limits established in the Speedy Trial Act of 1974.

8. Describe what constitutes a fair trial versus a free press.

9. Discuss the arguments for and against televising court proceedings.

10. Explain the jury selection process.

11. Describe several U.S. Supreme Court cases related to the use of peremptory challenges.

12. Describe the major stages in a criminal trial from the opening statements through sentencing.

13. Specify the stage of appeals where an indigent defendant retains the right to counsel.

14. Explain the importance of the "proof beyond a reasonable doubt" standard.

CHAPTER SUMMARY

Even though proportionately few cases are actually tried by juries, the trial process remains a focal point in the criminal justice system. The right to trial provides the defendant with a very important legal option. During the trial stage, the accused is protected by a number of constitutional rights.

The **Sixth Amendment** guarantees the defendant the right to a public trial by a jury of one(s) peers, although this right is frequently waived. The Sixth Amendment also provides the right to confront witnesses against you. The defendant has a fundamental right to counsel, but may choose to exercise the right to self-representation and proceed *pro se*. A speedy and fair trial are also guaranteed by the U.S. Constitution and various amendments to it.

The right to a fair trial has often been balanced against the First Amendment free press protection. While the U.S. Supreme Court has firmly established that criminal trials must remain public, the increasing issue is the allowance of electronic media coverage. While in federal court the use of television cameras, video recorders, and still photography has been banned, in most jurisdictions such coverage is at the discretion of the judge.

The **criminal trial** is a structured **adversary proceeding** where both the prosecution and defense follow specific procedures and argue the merits of their case before the judge and/or jury. A key step in the criminal trial process is the jury selection. During the process of *voir dire*, the prosecution and the defense can eliminate prospective jurors through **challenges for cause** and a limited number of **peremptory challenges**. The U.S. Supreme Court has sought to ensure compliance with the constitutional mandate for an **impartial jury**, through decisions such as *Batson v. Kentucky* which sought to eliminate racial discrimination in jury selection.

After jury selection, the trial proceeds through opening statements by each side, presentation of the evidence by the prosecutor and the defense attorney, and closing arguments. **Directed verdicts**, **rebuttals** by the state and **surrebuttals** by the defense are generally included in this process. After closing arguments, the judge will instruct, or *charge*, the jury on the applicable principles of law. In reaching their **verdict**, the jury must bear in mind that the criminal process requires **proof beyond a reasonable doubt** for each element of the offense. If the jury reaches a guilty verdict, the **sentence** will normally be imposed by the trial judge. In most jurisdictions, the defendant has an automatic right to **appeal** a conviction. If a defendant loses a direct first appeal, he or she can seek a discretionary appeal to a higher court, but if indigent, does so without the benefit of provided counsel.

Chapter 12

KEY TERMS AND CONCEPTS

Adjudication

Continuance

Six-Person Jury

Reasonable Doubt

In re Winship

Adversary Proceeding

Sixth Amendment

Jury Trial

Pro se

Faretta v. California

Speedy Trial

Cross-Examination

Batson v. Kentucky

Directed Verdict

Surrebuttal

Verdict

Sentence

In forma pauperis

Apodica v. Oregon

Sequestration

Klopfer v. North Carolina

Speedy Trial Act

First Amendment

Charge

Voir dire

Challenges for Cause

Peremptory Challenges

Bench Trials

Direct Examination

Real Evidence

Rebuttal Evidence

Venire

Hung Jury

Habeas Corpus

Preponderance of the Evidence

Fourteenth Amendment

Powell v. Alabama

Baldwin v. New York

FILL-IN REVIEW

1.   The _____ stage of the criminal justice process begins with a fact-finding hearing which seeks to determine the truth of the facts of a case before the court; this process is usually referred to as the _____ trial.

2.   Fewer than _____ percent of all defendants ever reach the trial stage.

3.   The defendant has the right to choose whether the trial will be before a _____ or _____.

4.   Although the _____ Amendment to the U.S. Constitution guarantees the defendant the right to a jury trial, the defendant can and often does _____ this right.

5.   In the case of *Baldwin v. New York*, the U.S. Supreme Court held that a defendant has a right to a _____ trial when he faces a prison sentence of _____ months or more.

6.   In the case of _____ v. _____, the U.S. Supreme Court held that a six person jury in a criminal trial did not deprive a defendant of his constitutional right to a jury trial.

The Criminal Trial

7. Today, the _____ verdict remains the rule in most state jurisdictions and in the federal system.

8. The right to proceed _____ _____ is when the criminal defendant is guaranteed the right to be able to represent himself.

9. The *Faretta v. California* decision was based on the belief that the right to self- _____ finds support in the _____ Amendment.

10. When *pro se* defendants' actions are disorderly and disruptive, the court can _____ their right to _____.

11. The _____ _____ Act of 1974 guarantees the accused that the trial must be held within _____ days after the arraignment.

12. A fair trial is one before an _____ judge and/or _____, in an environment of judicial restraint, orderliness, and fair decision making.

13. According to the U.S. Supreme Court, _____ hearings have traditionally been open to the _____ and should remain so.

14. The criminal trial is a structured _____ proceeding where both the prosecution and the defense follow specific procedures and argue the _____ of their cases.

15. _____ are selected randomly in both civil and criminal cases from tax assessments or voter registration lists in each court jurisdiction; this list is called a _____ or jury array.

16. A _____ _____ proceeding involves the questioning of the jurors selected to determine their appropriateness to sit on the trial.

17. In addition to challenges for cause, both the prosecution and the defense are allowed _____ _____.

18. The Sixth Amendment provides for the right to a _____ and _____ trial by an _____ jury.

19. _____ evidence often consists of the exhibits for review by the jury.

20. A _____ verdict is a procedural device by means of which the _____ attorney asks the judge to order the jury to return a verdict of not guilty.

21.   In a criminal trial, the defendant is protected by the Fifth Amendment right to be free from
        _____ - _____ .

22.   If a jury cannot reach a verdict, the trial may result in a _____ _____ ,
        and the prosecutor then has to bring the defendant to trial again if he desires a
        _____ .

23.   The imposition of the criminal _____ is normally the responsibility of the
        trial _____ .

24.   A writ of _____ _____ seeks to determine the validity of a
        detention by asking the court to release the person or give legal reasons for the
        _____ .

25.   Proof beyond a _____ _____ is the standard required to
        convict a criminal defendant.

SELF TEST

True/False

26.   Defendants are seldom able to see and cross-examine all witnesses against them.

27.   According to *Baldwin v. New York*, a defendant has a constitutional right to a jury trial, even
        when the possible sentence is less than six months.

28.   The continuance is a frequently used disposition in which the court holds a case in abeyance,
        without a finding of guilty, in order to induce the accused to improve his behavior.

29.   Because only a small number of cases are actually tried by a jury, the trial process is no
        longer considered a central ingredient to the criminal justice system.

30.   The Sixth Amendment does not guarantee a criminal defendant the right to a speedy trial in
        federal prosecution.

31.   Today, most states and the federal government have statutes which fix the period of time in
        which an accused must be brought to trial.

32.   Public information about criminal trials, the judicial system, and other areas of government is
        an essential and indispensable characteristic of a free society.

33.   Trial by media violates a defendant's right to a fair trial.

34.   The right to a public trial is basically for the benefit of the accused.

35. Chief justice Rehnquist is in favor of televising Supreme Court proceedings.

36. Peremptory challenges are not limited by law.

37. All jurisdictions conduct trials in a generally similar fashion.

38. For the most part, present rules dictate that the prosecutor is entitled to offer an opening statement first.

39. Opening statements are often only used in bench trials where juries are not employed.

40. The case of *Chandler v. Florida* makes it possible for all serious crimes and U.S. Supreme Court cases to be televised.

41. The primary test for the admissibility of evidence in a criminal or civil proceeding is relevance.

42. A directed verdict is a procedural device in which the prosecutor asks the judge to order the jury to return a verdict of guilty as charged.

43. Over the last decade, criminal appeals have decreased in almost every state and the federal courts.

44. Jurors often have a poor understanding of the judges instruction.

45. The case of *In re Winship* held that both state and federal court systems were bound to grant public trials to criminal defendants.

MULTIPLE CHOICE

46. Under the Speedy Trial Act of 1974, from the point of arrest the accused must be brought to trial within _____ days in the federal system.

    a. 30
    b. 60
    c. 100
    d. 150

47. Which of the following cases determined that the accused is entitled to a jury trial when the possible sentence is six months or longer.

    a. *Duncan v. Louisiana*
    b. *Williams v. Florida*
    c. *Baldwin v. New York*
    d. *Gideon v. Wainwright*

Chapter 12

48. In which of the following ways may a fair trial become violated.

    a.   hostile courtroom crowd
    b.   improper pressure on the witness
    c.   behavior that produces prejudice toward the accused
    d.   all of the above

49. In _____ v. _____, the Supreme Court clearly established that criminal trials must remain public.

    a.   *Press-Enterprise Co. v. Superior Court*
    b.   *Nebraska Press Association v. Stuart*
    c.   *Richmond Newspapers Inc. v. Virginia*
    d.   *Gannett Co. v. De Pasquale*

50. Which of the following is the initial list from which jurors are selected:

    a.   *voir dire*
    b.   *venire*
    c.   *pro se*
    d.   jury list

51. The process by which all persons selected as potential jurors are questioned by both the prosecution and defense is called:

    a.   *venire*
    b.   *pro se*
    c.   *voir dire*
    d.   directed questioning

52. The case of _____ v. _____ prevents an element of racial discrimination from entering into the trial stage of justice, and yet preserves the use of the peremptory challenge.

    a.   *Powell v. Alabama*
    b.   *Williams v. Florida*
    c.   *Barker v. Wingo*
    d.   *Batson v. Kentucky*

53. What the witness says, heard, or touched himself is put forth as which of the following:

    a.   evidence
    b.   testimony
    c.   examination
    d.   opinion

54. Which type of evidence is often inferred or indirectly used to prove a fact in question.

   a.   circumstantial
   b.   indirect
   c.   imaginary
   d.   both a and b

55. Who generally enters a motion for a directed verdict.

   a.   defense
   b.   prosecution
   c.   judge
   d.   both a and b

56. In a criminal trial when the judge instructs the jury as to the principles of law, this is known as which of the following:

   a.   charge
   b.   directs
   c.   surrebuttal
   d.   hung jury

57. Once the charge is given to the jury, they retire to deliberate upon which of the following:

   a.   sentence
   b.   verdict
   c.   conviction
   d.   recommendation

58. When the defendant is granted counsel at public expense because the court believes that he or she has meritorious appal, this is known as which of the following:

   a.   *in loco parentis*
   b.   *pro se*
   c.   *voir dire*
   d.   *in forma pauperis*

59. Which U.S. Supreme Court case established that peremptory challenges may not be used to strike down potential jurors solely on the basis of gender.

   a.   *Batson v. Kentucky*
   b.   *J.E.B. v. Alabama*
   c.   *Lockhart v. McCree*
   d.   *Chandler v. Florida*

Chapter 12

60.   Which of the following types of appeal are based on trial court errors.

   a.   direct appeals
   b.   federal court reviews
   c.   both a and b
   d.   neither a nor b

61.   Which U.S. Supreme Court case established the constitutionality of less than unanimous juries in noncapital cases.

   a.   *Apodica v. Oregon*
   b.   *Williams v. Florida*
   c.   *Baldwin v. New York*
   d.   *Maryland v. Craig*

MATCHING

62.   *Faretta v. California*

63.   *In re Winship*

64.   *Batson v. Kentucky*

65.   *Baldwin v. New York*

66.   *Klopfer v. North Carolina*

67.   *Maryland v. Craig*

68.   *Douglas v. California*

A.   Use of peremptory challenges

B.   Right to a speedy trial

C.   Right to self-representation

D.   Proof beyond a reasonable doubt

E.   Right to a jury trial

F.   Right to counsel on appeal

G.   Closed-circuit testimony

ESSAY QUESTIONS

69. Discuss the significance of the U.S. Supreme Court cases in *Baldwin v. New York* and *Batson v. Kentucky*.

70. What are the four primary purposes of the right to a speedy trial? What factors must be considered in determining whether or not this right has been violated?

71. Do you feel that criminal trials should be televised? Explain.

72. Explain the difference between challenges for cause and peremptory challenges in the jury selection process.

73. In your opinion, what is the importance of the reasonable doubt standard for establishing guilt?

74. Outline the major stages in a criminal trial. Explain why you would rather have a bench or jury trial.

CHAPTER TWELVE ANSWER SECTION

FILL-IN REVIEW

1. adjudication, criminal
2. five
3. judge, jury
4. Sixth, waive
5. jury, six
6. *Williams v. Florida*
7. unanimous
8. *pro se*
9. representation, Sixth
10. terminate, amendment
11. Speedy Trial, 60
12. impartial, jury
13. preliminary, public
14. adversarial, merits
15. Jurors, *venire*
16. *voir dire*
17. peremptory challenges
18. speedy, public, impartial
19. Real
20. directed, defense
21. self-incrimination
22. hung jury, conviction
23. sentence, judge
24. habeas corpus, incarceration
25. reasonable doubt

SELF TEST

True/False

26.	F	36.	F
27.	F	37.	T
28.	T	38.	T
29.	F	39.	F
30.	F	40.	F
31.	T	41.	T
32.	T	42.	F
33.	T	43.	F
34.	T	44.	T
35.	F	45.	F

MULTIPLE CHOICE

46.	C	54.	D
47.	C	55.	A
48.	D	56.	A
49.	C	57.	B
50.	B	58.	D
51.	C	59.	B
52.	D	60.	C
53.	B	61.	A

MATCHING

62. C
63. D
64. A
65. E
66. B
67. G
68. F

13 Punishment and Sentencing

LEARNING OBJECTIVES

1. Outline the history of punishment and the rise of the prison system.

2. List and describe the different objectives of criminal sentencing.

3. Describe the different kind of sentences which can be imposed on a convicted offender.

4. Distinguish between a concurrent and consecutive sentence.

5. Differentiate among indeterminate, determinate, mandatory, presumptive, and structured sentencing.

6. Discuss habitual criminal statutes and related U.S. Supreme Court decisions.

7. Explain the meaning of disparity in the sentencing process, and list some possible extralegal factors.

8. Provide several arguments for and against the death penalty.

9. Explain the importance of the following cases regarding the death penalty: *Furman v. Georgia*, *Gregg v. Georgia*, and *McLesky v. Kemp*.

10. Describe the findings of several studies regarding capital punishment and deterrence.

CHAPTER SUMMARY

Punishment and sentencing has undergone different phases throughout the history of Western civilization. In early Greek and Roman civilizations, the most common state-administered punishment was banishment or exile. During the feudal period, the main emphasis of criminal law and punishment was on maintaining public order. The development of the common law in the eleventh century brought some standardization to penal punishments. However, capital and corporal punishments were still widely used.

Today, after a defendant has been found guilty of a crime, the state has the right to impose a **criminal sanction**. The process in which the nature and extent of punishment is decided upon is referred to as the **sentencing process**. The objectives of criminal sentencing today can usually be grouped into several distinct areas: **general deterrence, incapacitation, specific deterrence, retribution/desert,** and **rehabilitation**. The concept of **restitution** means that the convicted criminal must pay back the victim for his or her loss, the justice system for the costs of processing the case, and society for any disruption they may have caused.

Sentencing options where convicted offenders may be sent to prison include **indeterminate, determinate, presumptive, mandatory,** and **structured** sentencing. Each of these schemes is based on philosophical differences about punishment, rehabilitation, and justice. **Habitual criminal statutes**, are also used in many jurisdictions, mandating that people who have been convicted and served time for multiple felony offenses receive either an enhanced punishment for the current crime or a mandatory life term without possibility of parole.

Because a wide variety of sentencing practices are utilized, concern has developed regarding judicial discretion and the degree to which **disparity** exists in the sentencing process. Control over the length of sentences has shifted in some large jurisdictions from the judicial and administrative to the legislative branches of government. More than half the states now employ sentencing schemes which are legislatively determined and insulated from judicial or administrative discretion.

The most severe sentence used in our nation is capital punishment. Applied extensively throughout American history, there have been more than 14,500 confirmed executions. Currently there are about 2,700 people on death row. The use of capital punishment has been hotly debated, with many common arguments given for the retention as well as the abolition of its use. In 1972, the U.S. Supreme Court in *Furman v. Georgia* decided that the discretionary imposition of the death penalty was **cruel and unusual punishment** under the Eighth and Fourteenth Amendments of the Constitution. Then, in 1976, the U.S. Supreme Court, in *Gregg v. Georgia*, found valid the Georgia statute which held that a finding by the jury of at least one "aggravating circumstance" out of ten was required before pronouncing the death penalty in murder cases. In *McLesky v. Kemp*, the U.S. Supreme Court ruled that the evidence of racial patterns in capital sentencing was not persuasive, absent a finding of racial bias in the immediate case. Considerable empirical research has been carried out on the effectiveness of capital punishment as a deterrent, almost all of which confirms that there is no deterrent effect. In fact, some research points to a **brutalizing effect**, suggesting that executions actually increase murder rates by raising the general violence level in society.

KEY TERMS AND CONCEPTS

Criminal Sanction	Mandatory Minimum Sentences
Sentencing Process	Disparity
Sentencing Disparity	Presumptive Sentencing
Wergild	Sentencing Guidelines
Wite	Structured Sentencing
Bot	Advisory Guideline
Poor Laws	Mandatory Guideline
Penitentiaries	Base Penalty
General Deterrence	Habitual Criminal Statutes
Incapacitation	*Solem v. Helm*
Specific Deterrence	Extra-Legal Factors
Recidivism	Capital Punishment
Retribution	*Furman v. Georgia*
Restitution	Cruel and Unusual Punishment
Rehabilitation	Eighth Amendment
Just Desert	Fourteenth Amendment
Sentencing Strategies	*Gregg v. Georgia*
Concurrent Sentence	*McKesky v. Kemp*
Consecutive Sentence	Death-Qualified Juries
Indeterminate Sentences	*Lockhart v. McCree*
Determinate Sentences	Impact Studies
Harmelin v. Michigan	Contiguous State Analysis
Rummel v. Estelle	Time Series
Stanford v. Kentucky	Brutalization Effect
Clemens v. Mississippi	Selective Incapacitation
Good Time	Contextual Discrimination

FILL-IN REVIEW

1. The process in which the nature and extent of punishment is decided on is referred to
   _____ .

2. A period of confinement in a state or federal prison, jail, or community based treatment
   facility is known as _____ .

3. _____ laws which developed at the end of the _____
   century, required the poor, vagrants, and vagabonds be put to work in public or private
   enterprise.

Punishment and Sentencing

4. _____ of corrections were developed to make it convenient for petty law violators to be assigned to work details.

5. By 1820, long periods of incarceration in walled institutions called reformatories or _____ began to replace _____ punishment in England and the United States.

6. _____ deterrence refers to the ability of criminal punishments to convince the convicted criminal that _____ would not be in their best interest.

7. _____ based sentencing evaluates the weight of the criminal act, not the needs of the offender or community.

8. The concept of ___ _____ mandates the convicted criminal pay back the victim for his or her loss, the justice system for the costs of processing the case, and society for any disruption that may have been caused.

9. If a defendant is convicted of two or more charges, and is serving a _____ sentence, the sentence is completed after the _____ term has been served.

10. If a defendant is serving a _____ sentence, the defendant would begin serving time for the second charge at the _____ of the first.

11. In the _____ fixed model of sentencing the legislature determines a general range of prison sentences for a given crime and the sentencing _____ then determines a sentence within that range.

12. Regarding the nation's sentencing policy, control over the length of sentences has shifted from the _____ to the _____ branches of government.

13. An _____ sentence gives convicted offenders a light _____ sentence that must be served and a lengthy _____ sentence that is the outer boundary of the time that can be served.

14. A _____ sentence is one in which the duration of the offender's prison stay is determined by the _____ sentence that is the outer boundary of the time that can be served.

15. _____ sentences allow the legislature to set an expected sentence range for a particular crime, with judges sentencing within the prescribed range unless they give a _____, in writing, justifying any action above or below the sentencing guidelines.

16. Sentencing _____ outline the elements of a _____ and provide pre-determined weights to the elements, which then leads to the selection of a most appropriate sentence.

17. _____ sentencing generally limits the judge's _____ power to impose any disposition but that authorized by the legislature.

18. _____ criminal statutes mandate that people convicted of multiple felony offenses be given mandatory _____ terms or sentence _____.

19. In 1972, the U.S. Supreme Court in *Furman v. Georgia* decided that the discretionary imposition of the death penalty was _____ and _____ punishment under the _____ and _____ Amendments of the Constitution.

20. In 1976, the U.S. Supreme Court ruled in *Gregg v. Georgia* that the statute which held that the finding by a jury of at least one "_____ _____" out of ten is required in pronouncing the death penalty in murder cases.

21. The U.S. Supreme Court, in *McLesky v. Kemp*, discounted the research evidence of racial patterns in _____ sentencing when there was no finding of racial bias in the immediate case.

22. _____ series studies look at the long term association between capital sentencing and _____.

23. The _____ effect is when people prone to violence identify with the executioner and not the executed offender in the use of the death penalty.

SELF TEST

True/False

24. In early Greek and Roman civilizations, the most common form of state-administered punishment was banishment or exile.

25. The "just desert" philosophy of punishment holds that criminal sentences should be proportional to the seriousness of an offenders' criminal act.

26. The length of time served by an inmate is controlled by the correctional agency in indeterminate sentences.

Punishment and Sentencing

27. Prosecutors oppose the use of sentencing guidelines because they result in shorter prison terms.

28. Mandatory sentencing generally limits the judge's discretionary power to impose any disposition but that authorized by the legislature.

29. If an offender is serving a consecutive sentence for two charges, the sentence is completed after the longest term has been served.

30. A report by the National Council of Crime and Delinquency found that the use of mandatory sentences in Florida has led to a reduction of inmates in the correctional system.

31. There is no evidence that women are less likely to receive incarceration sentences than men.

32. Research on disparity in sentencing has failed to show a definitive pattern of racial discrimination.

33. There have been more than 20,000 confirmed executions in America.

34. "Death-qualified" juries are ones in which any person opposed in concept to capital punishment has been removed during *voir dire*.

35. The U.S. Supreme Court appears committed to abolishing the death penalty.

36. Studies have indicated that capital punishment has a significant effect as a deterrent measure on the murder rate.

37. More than 70 percent of prison inmates have had prior convictions and more than half of all inmates return to prison within three years of their release.

38. Habitual criminal statutes mandate that people convicted of multiple felony offenses be given mandatory life terms without the possibility of parole.

39. Most research studies have found that the publicity about executions have little influence on murder rates.

40. Though discretion has been restricted, research indicates that income, gender, and race still influence sentencing.

41. Federal sentencing guidelines suggest a harsher punishment for crack cocaine than for powdered cocaine.

42. It is expected that sentence enhancements and sentencing guidelines will reduce the amount of prison time served in the future.

Chapter 13

MULTIPLE CHOICE

43.   In which of the following models does the state legislature determine the penalty for a specific crime, and all people convicted of that crime receive that sentence.

      a.   judicially fixed
      b.   legislatively fixed
      c.   administrative
      d.   all of the above

44.   In the _____ model of sentencing, the legislature determines a general range of prison sentences and the sentencing judge determines a sentence within that range.

      a.   judicially fixed
      b.   legislatively fixed
      c.   administrative
      d.   none of the above

45.   Indeterminate sentences are the heart of which of the following models of corrections.

      a.   rehabilitation
      b.   punishment
      c.   retribution
      d.   reintegration

46.   Which is the predominant form of sentencing used in the criminal process today.

      a.   indeterminate sentencing
      b.   determinate sentencing
      c.   mandatory sentencing
      d.   both b and c

47.   Today about _____ states use indeterminate sentencing.

      a.   10
      b.   20
      c.   30
      d.   40

48.   Which of the following are objectives of presumptive sentencing strategies.

      a.   to reduce sentencing disparity
      b.   to limit judicial discretion without completely eliminating it
      c.   to impose a sentence which the offender is required to serve
      d.   all of the above

49. Under indeterminate sentencing, the actual length of time served by the inmate is controlled by which of the following.

   a.   judge
   b.   corrections agency
   c.   legislature
   d.   both a and b

50. Which of the following is an approach to sentencing which allows the legislature to set a minimum and maximum term and the judge to set a fixed or determinate sentence within this rate.

   a.   mandatory sentencing
   b.   flat sentencing
   c.   indeterminate sentencing
   d.   presumptive sentencing

51. One of the major concerns resulting from judicial discretion is the degree to which _____ exists in the sentencing process.

   a.   distress
   b.   duress
   c.   disparity
   d.   difficulty

52. In _____ v. _____, the U.S. Supreme Court ruled that a sentence of imprisonment can be considered cruel and unusual if it is disproportionate to the crime committed.

   a.   *Gregg v. Georgia*
   b.   *Furman v. Georgia*
   c.   *Solem v. Helm*
   d.   *Profitt v. Florida*

53. Which of the following are extralegal factors.

   a.   the crime itself
   b.   the charge filed
   c.   the age of the defendant
   d.   none of the above are extra legal factors

54. Which of the following cases determined that a convicted offender can be sentenced to death when one or more "aggravating circumstances" were involved.

    a.   *Furman v. Georgia*
    b.   *Gregg v. Georgia*
    c.   *Roberts v. Louisiana*
    d.   *Profitt v. Florida*

55. The U.S. Supreme Court decided that the discretionary imposition of the death penalty was cruel and unusual in which of the following cases.

    a.   *Gregg v. Georgia*
    b.   *Jurek v. Texas*
    c.   *McGinnis v. Royster*
    d.   *Furman v. Georgia*

56. The case of _____ v. _____ stated that racial bias must be found in the immediate case before racial pattern evidence in capital sentencing could be considered persuasive.

    a.   *Jurek v. Texas*
    b.   *McLesky v. Kemp*
    c.   *Roberts v. Roberts*
    d.   *Black v. Smith*

57. In_____ v. _____, the U.S. Supreme Court ruled that removing anti-capital punishment jurors does not violate the Sixth Amendment provision that juries must represent a fair cross section of the community.

    a.   *Furman v. Georgia*
    b.   *Lockhart v. McCree*
    c.   *Solem v. Helm*
    d.   none of the above

58. Approximately _____ percent of Americans surveyed in the 1990's approved of the use of capital punishment.

    a.   10
    b.   25
    c.   50
    d.   80

59. According to the U.S. Supreme Court, which is the minimum age limit for imposition of the death penalty.

    a.   15 years old
    b.   16 years old
    c.   17 years old
    d.   18 years old

60. Which of the following ideology focuses on the potential risk to society and attempts to predict future criminal behavior.

    a.   incapacitation
    b.   deterrence
    c.   retribution
    d.   rehabilitation

61. Approximately _____ of black males age 20-29 are under some form of correctional care today.

    a.   one-fifth
    b.   one-quarter
    c.   one-third
    d.   one-half

62. How many states allow capital punishment for murder and other serious crimes.

    a.   18
    b.   24
    c.   36
    d.   45

MATCHING

63.   Determinate Sentence   A.   Excludes probation or parole

64.   Indeterminate Sentence   B.   Fits offender's needs

65.   Habitual Offender Statutes   C.   Some judicial discretion

66.   Presumptive Sentence   D.   Fixed term

67.   Mandatory Sentence   E.   Life term without parole

ESSAY QUESTIONS

68. Briefly discuss the objectives of sentencing.

69. Provide an example of the following types of sentences: indeterminate, determinate, mandatory, and presumptive.

70. Discuss how sentencing guidelines are used. Do you believe they provide equity in the sentencing process? Why or why not?

71. Discuss several reasons why disparity exists in sentencing today.

72. List and discuss several arguments for and against the death penalty.

73. What was the significance of the U.S. Supreme Court's decisions regarding capital punishment in 1972 and 1976? What does the research indicate regarding executions and deterrence?

CHAPTER THIRTEEN ANSWER SECTION

FILL-IN REVIEW

1. sentencing
2. incarceration
3. Poor, 16th
4. Houses
5. penitentiaries, physical
6. Specific, recidivism
7. Desert
8. restitution
9. concurrent, longest
10. consecutive, completion
11. judicially, judge
12. administrative, legislative
13. indeterminate, minimum, maximum
14. determinate, judiciary
15. Presumptive, reason
16. guidelines, crime
17. Mandatory, discretionary
18. Habitual, life, enhancements
19. cruel, unusual, Eighth, Fourteenth
20. aggravating circumstance
21. capital
22. Time, murder
23. brutalization

SELF TEST

True/False

24.	T	34.	T
25.	T	35.	F
26.	T	36.	F
27.	F	37.	T
28.	T	38.	F
29.	F	39.	T
30.	F	40.	T
31.	F	41.	T
32.	T	42.	F
33.	F		

MULTIPLE CHOICE

43.	B	53.	C
44.	A	54.	B
45.	A	55.	D
46.	A	56.	B
47.	C	57.	B
48.	D	58.	D
49.	B	59.	B
50.	D	60.	A
51.	C	61.	C
52.	C	62.	C

MATCHING

63.	D
64.	B
65.	E
66.	C
67.	A

14 Probation and Intermediate Sanctions

LEARNING OBJECTIVES

1. Describe the philosophy and history of probation and the development of probation in the United States.

2. Explain the extent of probation in the United States, and specify an approximate "successful" completion rate.

3. List several criteria which are used in considering a probation sentence.

4. Describe the four primary duties of a probation officer.

5. Explain the significance of pre-sentence investigations.

6. Define the probationer's limited right to counsel in revocation proceedings using U.S. Supreme Court case law.

7. Define forfeiture and discuss the holdings of the U.S. Supreme Court cases of *Austin v. U.S.* and *Alexander v. U.S.*

8. Distinguish between financial and community-service restitution.

9. Define shock probation and split sentencing.

10. Discuss intensive Probation Supervision (IPS), house arrest, electronic monitoring and Residential Community Corrections (RCC).

CHAPTER SUMMARY

Probation, the practice of maintaining offenders in the community under supervision of court authority, can be traced historically to the traditions of English common law. The modern concept of probation was pioneered by **John Augustus**, and has remained the sentence of choice in American courts. The philosophy behind probation is that the average offender is not actually a dangerous criminal or a menace to society.

Probation usually involves suspension of the offender's sentence in return for the promise of good behavior in the community and/or the fulfillment of other conditions determined by the sentencing judge.

Probation officers are usually charged with four primary tasks: **investigation**, **intake**, **diagnosis**, and **treatment supervision**. The investigation and evaluation of defendants coming before the court for sentencing is a key responsibility, as are the recommendations in the probation officer's **pre-sentence investigation**. Numerous factors influence the probation officer's investigation report, especially the nature of the current offense and the offender's criminal history.

Probationers enjoy fewer constitutional protections than other citizens including limitations on Fifth Amendment protection against self-incrimination and unreasonable search and seizure. Probationers have been granted the right to counsel at probation revocation proceedings and the right to a formal revocation hearing after an informal hearing to determine whether probable cause for revocation exists.

The current United States trend is "probation plus," the addition of restrictive penalties and/or conditions to community service orders. These programs are known as **intermediate sanctions** and include programs that are typically administered by probation departments such as: **intensive probation supervision**; **house arrest**; **electronic monitoring**; **restitution orders**; **shock probation/split sentences**; and **residential community corrections**. While it is too soon to determine whether these programs are successful, they provide the hope of being low cost, high security alternatives to traditional corrections.

KEYS TERMS AND CONCEPTS

Probation
Judicial Reprieve
Recognizance
Sureties
John Augustus
Revocation
Suspended Sentence
Risk Classification
Revocation
Gagnon v. Scarpelli
Day Fees
Alternative Sanctions
Intermediate Sanctions
Fines
Day Fines
Tate v. Short
Forfeiture
Racketeer Influenced and Corrupt
Organization Act (RICO)
Forfeiture
Alexander v. United States

Restitution
Chief Probation Officer (CPO)
Probation Officers
Intake
Diagnosis
Pre-sentence Investigations
Monetary Restitution
Community-Service Restitution
Split Sentencing
Shock Probation
Intensive Probation Supervision (IPS)
Diversion
Control
Reintegration
House Arrest
Electronic Monitoring (EM)
Residential Community Corrections (RCC)
Nexus
Day Reporting Centers (DRC's)
Zero Tolerance
Austin v. United States
"Son of Sam" Laws

FILL-IN REVIEW

1. The most common alternative sanction is _____, which involves maintaining an _____ in the community under a set of behavioral rules created and administered by judicial authority.

2. _____ were people who made themselves responsible for the behavior of the offender after they were _____.

3. _____ _____ of Boston is usually credited with organizing the modern probation concept.

4. The philosophy of probation is that the average offender is not actually a _____ criminal or a menace to _____.

5. Each probationary sentence is for a _____ period of time, depending on the seriousness of the offense and the _____ law of the jurisdiction.

Chapter 14

6.   The extensive use of probation is probably a reflection of its low relatively
      _____, as compared to the housing of inmates in prison.

7.   Many states have attempted to control judicial _____ by creating
      _____ for granting probation.

8.   A probationary sentence is usually viewed as an act of _____ on the part of the
      court, and is reflective of the _____ aspects of the criminal justice system.

9.   In addition to _____ rules, judges may legally impose restrictions on a
      probationer tailored to fit his or her individual needs and to protect _____
      from additional harm.

10.   In the typical probation department, the _____ probation officer sets
      policy, supervises hiring, determines what training should be emphasized, and may
      personally discuss with or recommend sentencing to the judge.

11.   _____ is a process by which probation officers _____
      cases that have been summoned to the court for initial appearances.

12.   _____ is the analysis of the probationer's personality and the subsequent
      development of a personality _____ that may be helpful in treating the
      offender.

13.   The treatment function is a product of both the _____ and
      _____ aspects of probation.

14.   _____ - _____ _____ are used by the court in
      making decisions regarding whether to grant probation, incarcerate, or use other forms of
      treatment.

15.   _____ _____ involves classifying and assigning cases to
      a level and type of probation based on the clients perceived needs and the risk they represent
      to the community.

16.   The U.S. Supreme Court case of *Gagnon v. Scarpelli* held that both probationers and
      parolees have a constitutionally limited right to _____ in
      _____ proceedings.

17.   _____ are monetary payments imposed on an _____ as
      an intermediate punishment for their criminal acts.

18.   The practice of seizing expensive property by law enforcement agencies for even small
      amounts of illegal substances is known as _____ _____.

19. _____requires defendants to either pay back the victims of crime or serve the community for their _____ acts.

20. Combining probation with jail sentences is known as _____ _____ or_____ _____.

21. _____ _____ requires offenders to spend extended periods of time in their home as an alternative to a _____ sentence.

22. _____ _____ helps assure sentencing authorities that arrestees are actually home during their assigned times during house arrest.

23. _____sanctions, or "_____ plus," add restrictive penalties and/or conditions to community service orders.

SELF TEST

True/False

24. About two-thirds of all adults under some form of correctional supervision are on probation.

25. The use of probation has been decreasing in the United States.

26. Private prisons are now common in America.

27. The courts will not allow the conditions of probation to include warrantless searches or drug testing if no evidence of substance abuse existed prior to the probationary period.

28. Probationary conditions may not infringe on constitutional rights.

29. Intake is most common in the juvenile justice process, but may also be employed in adult felony cases.

30. Probation officers seem more interested today in treating clients than in controlling their behavior.

31. At the conclusion of most pre-sentence investigations, a recommendation is made to the presiding judge which reflects the department's sentencing posture on the case at hand.

32. The right to counsel in revocation proceedings differs for probationers and parolees.

33. Intermediate sanctions help meet the need for developing community sentences that are fair, equitable, proportional, and cost effective.

34. An offender's probation cannot be revoked unless he commits another crime.

35. Forfeiture involves the seizure of goods and instrumentalities related to the commission or outcome of a criminal act.

36. The original enthusiasm for the concept of restitution has been dampened by concern that it has not lived up to its promises as an alternative to incarceration.

37. Restitution programs normally require offenders to pay back victims of crime or perform community service as a condition of probation.

38. In some state jurisdictions, jail terms can actually be a condition of probation.

39. Today, the community correctional facility serves as a vehicle to provide intermediate sanctions as well as a pre-release center for those about to be paroled from the prison system.

40. The crimes and criminal records of twenty-five percent of all probationers is virtually indistinguishable from those of their incarcerated counterparts.

41. The least successful probationers tend to be women with stable marriages, between education, and full or part-time employment.

42. According to recent decisions by the U.S. Supreme Court, seizures of property need not be proportional to the seriousness of the crime in civil forfeitures.

MULTIPLE CHOICE

43. Who was the originator of the modern concept of probation.

    a. David Rothman
    b. O.W. Wilson
    c. John Augustus
    d. none of the above

44. The practice of _____ enabled convicted offenders to remain free if they agree to enter into a debt obligation with the state.

    a. probation
    b. recognizance
    c. judicial reprieve
    d. sureties

Probation and Intermediate Sanctions

45. There are approximately _____ adult probation agencies in the United States.

    a. 500
    b. 1,000
    c. 2,000
    d. 5,000

46. Which of the following is a process by which probation officers interview cases which have been summoned to the court for an initial appearance.

    a. intake
    b. diagnosis
    c. investigation
    d. diversion

47. The analysis of the probationer's personality and the subsequent development of personality profile which may be helpful in treating the offender is known as which of the following.

    a. diversion
    b. diagnosis
    c. determination
    d. discretion

48. Staff officers in probation are usually charged with which of the following duties.

    a. intake
    b. diagnosis
    c. treatment supervision
    d. all of the above

49. In general about _____ percent of all felons and misdemeanants successfully complete their probation

    a. 20
    b. 40
    c. 70
    d. 80

50. Which of the following cases held that both probationers and parolees have a constitutionally limited right to counsel.

    a. *Gagnon v. Scarpelli*
    b. *Minnesota v. Murphy*
    c. *Mempa v. Rhay*
    d. *Morrissey v. Brewer*

51. Which of the following programs are intermediate sanctions, typically administered by probation departments.

    a. house arrest
    b. electronic monitoring
    c. restitution orders
    d. all of the above

52. During the course of a probationary term, a violation of the rules of probation or the commission of a new crime can cause probation to be _____.

    a. renewed
    b. revoked
    c. reorganized
    d. recalled

53. Incarcerating offenders who are financially unable to pay a fine was ruled discrimination against the poor in the U.S. Supreme Court case of _____ .

    a. *Tate v. Short*
    b. *Indigents v. Feds*
    c. *Sharp v. Tatum*
    d. *Chase v. Manhattan*

54. Shock probation has been praised for which of the following reasons.

    a. mitigating the purpose of probation
    b. providing a way of reducing the prison population
    c. providing a way of reducing the costs of corrections
    d. both b and c

55. The goals of intensive probation supervision include which of the following.

    a. diversion
    b. control
    c. reintegration
    d. all of the above

56. What percentage of convicted felons receive probation.

    a. 35%
    b. 25%
    c. 15%
    d. 5%

57. In what percentage of all criminal convictions is probation utilized.

    a. 0-20%
    b. 20-40%
    c. 40-60%
    d. 60-80%

58. Financial restitution is ordered in about _____ percent of all probation cases.

    a. 10
    b. 20
    c. 30
    d. 40

59. Most probationers are young, _____, unmarried and under-educated males.

    a. white
    b. black
    c. hispanic
    d. no statistically significant difference in race

MATCHING

60. Restitution

A. Seizure of goods and instrumentalities of crime

61. Intake

B. Re-sentencing of an offender after a short prison stay

62. Diagnosis

C. Pay back victim or serve the community

63. Shock Probation

D. Interview of cases which have been summoned to the court

64. Investigation

E. An analysis of the probationer's personality

65. Forfeiture

F. Inquiry within the community to discover the factors related to the criminality of the offender

ESSAY QUESTIONS

66.   Why do many experts disapprove of combining probation with jail sentences and why do some courts allow it anyway?

67.   Discuss the major duties of a probation officer; should these be expanded or narrowed?

68.   Discuss the major reasons why a court may decide not to grant probation.

69.   Discuss the procedural safeguards for probation revocation; from what cases did these safeguards arise.

70.   Define intensive probation supervision, house arrest, electronic monitoring, and residential community corrections.

71.   Give several reasons why restitution should or should not be required of criminal offenders.

CHAPTER FOURTEEN ANSWER SECTION

FILL-IN REVIEW

1. probation, offender
2. Sureties, released
3. John Augustus
4. dangerous, society
5. fixed, statutory
6. cost
7. discretion, guidelines
8. mercy, rehabilitative
9. standard, society
10. chief, judge
11. Intake, interview
12. Diagnosis, profile
13. investigative, diagnostic
14. Pre-sentence investigations
15. Risk classification
16. counsel, revocation
17. Fines, offender
18. zero tolerance
19. Restitution, criminal
20. shock probation, split sentencing
21. House arrest, prison
22. Electronic monitoring
23. Intermediate, probation

SELF TEST

True/False

24.	T	34.	F
25.	F	35.	T
26.	T	36.	T
27.	T	37.	T
28.	F	38.	T
29.	F	39.	T
30.	T	40.	T
31.	T	41.	F
32.	F	42.	F
33.	T		

MULTIPLE CHOICE

43.	C	52.	B
44.	B	53.	A
45.	C	54.	D
46.	A	55.	C
47.	B	56.	B
48.	D	57.	D
49.	D	58.	C
50.	A	59.	A
51.	D		

MATCHING

60.	C
61.	D
62.	E
63.	B
64.	F
65.	A

15 Corrections: History, Institutions, and Populations

LEARNING OBJECTIVES

1. Define the historical significance and meaning of the freesystem, capital and corporal punishment.

2. Explain William Penn's contribution to correctional reform.

3. Differentiate between the operating philosophies of the Walnut Street Jail, the Auburn System, and Pennsylvania's Western and Eastern Penitentiaries.

4. Explain the significance of Z.R. Brockway and the Elmira Reformatory regarding correctional reform.

5. List the five primary purposes of the nation's jails.

6. Describe at least three major problems facing local jails.

7. Define "custodial convenience."

8. List at least three reasons for prison overcrowding and several ways such overcrowding may be alleviated.

9. Differentiate between ultramaximum, maximum, medium, and minimum security prisons.

10. Describe the characteristics of the average prison inmate.

11. Explain the concept of private business participation in corrections.

CHAPTER SUMMARY

When a person is convicted for a criminal offense, state and federal governments through their sentencing authority reserve the right to institutionally confine the offender for an extended period of time. The system of **secure corrections** comprises the entire range of treatment and/or punishment options available to the government, including **community residential centers**, **jails**, **reformatories**, and penal institutions or **prisons**. Felons may be placed in state or federal penitentiaries (prisons), which are usually isolated, fortress-like structures; misdemeanants are housed in county jails, sometimes called reformatories or houses of correction; and juvenile offenders have their own institutions, sometimes referred to as schools, camps, ranches or homes.

One of the greatest tragedies of our time is that correctional institutions do not seem to correct. They are, in most instances, overcrowded, understaffed, outdated warehouses for social outcasts. Although no completely accurate statement of the **recidivism** rate is available, it is estimated that more than half of all inmates will be back in prison within six years of their release. Despite the apparent lack of success experienced by penal institutions, great debates still range over the direction of their future operations. There are penal experts who maintain that jails and prisons are not really places for rehabilitation and treatment but should be used to keep dangerous offenders apart from society and give them the "just deserts" for their crimes. Despite the growth of this view, there still exists many penal experts who maintain that prisons can be useful places for offender rehabilitation; evident in flourishing education, vocational training, and treatment programs.

Today's correctional institutions can trace their development from European origins. Punishment methods developed in Europe were modified and improved by American colonists, most notably **William Penn**. He replaced torture and mutilation with imprisonment at hard labor, fines and forfeiture.

In 1816, New York developed the **Auburn Prison** where prisoners ate and worked in groups during the day and were separated at night. The congregate system is still widely used in our current penal institutions.

With the rise in prison population came the development of **prison industry**. Under **contract systems** prison officials sold inmate labor to private businesses. Under **convict-lease systems** the state leased prisoners to businesses for a fixed annual fee and relinquished supervision and control. Another system allowed prisoners to produce goods for the state's use.

Many abuses occurred in prisons leading to calls for reform. Z.R. Brockway, warden of the Elmira Reformatory, advocated a "new penology" including: individualized treatment, indeterminate sentencing, parole, elementary education and vocational training. Many such reforms reflected belief in rehabilitation and are still used today.

There are approximately 3,400 jails in the United States which serve many purposes, including: detaining accused offenders who cannot make or are not eligible for bail prior to trial; confining convicted offenders awaiting sentence and those convicted of misdemeanors; holding probationer and parolee violators who are awaiting a hearing; and housing felons when state prisons are overcrowded. Jails tend to be overcrowded and are usually administered under the concept of "**custodial convenience**," which involves giving inmates minimum standards of treatment and benefits, while controlling the cost of jail operations.

Closed correctional facilities, also known as prisons, are usually classified on three levels: **maximum**, **medium**, and **minimum security**; each with distinct characteristics. The significant rise in the prison population can be explained by the use of mandatory and determinate sentencing laws, high unemployment, and inability of offenders to post bail due to difficult economic times. One of the goals of correctional treatment is to **reintegrate** the offender back to society. With this goal in mind, the **community corrections** concept began to take hold in the 1960's, and includes innovative alternatives to incarceration, such as **halfway houses**, to which inmates are transferred just prior to their release into the community. Halfway houses are designed to bridge the gap between institutional living and the community.

One recent development has been privately run correctional institutions. These are jails and prisons operated by private companies which receive a fee for their services. There are some concerns about such institutions related to effectiveness, liability and service.

KEY TERMS AND CONCEPTS

Secure Corrections
Jails
Reformatories
Prisons
Hulks
John Howard
Walnut Street Jail
Penitentiary House
Tier System
Congregate System
Pennsylvania System
Auburn System
Contract System
Convict-Lease System
Z.R. Brockway
Recidivism
William Penn
Prisoners' Rights Movement

Medical Model
Reintegration
Custodial Convenience
Overcrowding
Maximum Security
Medium Security
Minimum Security
Maxi-Maxi Prisons
Farms
Camps
Shock Incarceration
Community Corrections
Halfway Houses
Private Corrections
Rehabilitation
Prison Industry
Sumners-Ashurst Act

Chapter 15

FILL-IN REVIEW

1.   The system of secure _____ includes the entire range of
        _____ and/or _____ options available to the government.

2.   Although no completely accurate statement of the _____ rate is available, it
        is estimated that more than _____ of all inmates return to prison within
        three years of their release.

3.   _____ _____ book, *The State of Prisons*, regarding the inhumane
        standards in the British penal system resulted in the Penitentiary Act in which Parliament
        limited the use of the death penalty, and made prison an alternative to physical punishment.

4.   The U.S. correctional system had its origin in Pennsylvania under the leadership of
        _____ _____ .

5.   In the Walnut Street Jail most prisoners were placed in _____ cells, where
        they remained in _____ and did not have the right to work.

6.   Regarding the Walnut Street Jail, the quarters that contained the solitary or separate cells
        were called the _____ house.

7.   The philosophy of the _____ system was crime prevention through fear of
        _____ and silent confinement.

8.   In 1818, Pennsylvania's Western Penitentiary developed a prison that placed each inmate in a
        _____ cell for the duration of their sentence.

9.   The Western Penitentiary was built in a _____, with the cells positioned
        along the _____ .

10.   Under the _____ - _____ system, the state leased its
        prisoners to a business for a fixed annual fee and gave up supervision and control.

11.   The greatest significance of Z.R. Brockway's contributions to the penal system was the
        injection of a degree of _____ into the industrial prison of the day.

12.   The _____ - _____ Act of 1940 made it a federal offense
        to transport interstate commerce goods made in prison for private use.

13.   The _____ _____ movement from 1960 to 1980 gained
        rights for inmates; including freedom of religion and speech, medical care, procedural due
        process and proper living conditions.

14. Because jails are almost always administered on a _____ level, there has been neither significant regulation of services nor development of a unified national policy to ensure adequate jail _____.

15. Jails are usually administered under the concept of "_____ _____" which involves giving inmates minimum _____ of treatment and benefits while controlling the cost of jail operations.

16. The most critical problems of jails is _____.

17. Prisons are generally organized or classified on three levels: _____, _____, or _____ security; and each has its own distinctive characteristics.

18. Some states have constructed _____ - _____ prisons to house the most predatory criminals.

19. The concept of _____ _____ is that short periods (90 to 180 days) of high intensity exercise and work will "shock" an inmate into going straight.

20. One of the goals of correctional treatment is to _____ the offender back into society.

21. A _____ house is a facility to which inmates are transferred just prior to their _____ into the community.

22. A new development in corrections is _____ participation in the correctional enterprise.

SELF TEST

True/False

23. Modern prisons are more suited to control, punishment, and security than to rehabilitation and treatment.

24. Correctional reform was first instituted in Europe.

25. The Walnut Street Jail instituted the congregate system, where most prisoners ate and worked in groups.

26. In the Auburn system, the key to prison discipline was hard work and silence.

27. The Pennsylvania system placed each inmate in a single cell and provided them with in-cell work.

28. The Auburn system was referred to as the congregate system, since most prisoners ate and worked in groups.

29. In the seventeenth and eighteenth centuries, discipline was generally some form of physical torture.

30. The Pennsylvania system eventually prevailed in the United States; many of its features are still used today.

31. More than 1 million women are admitted to jail annually.

32. Since 1983, the percentage of men in jail has increased at a rate double that of females.

33. Approximately 900 people die in jail each year; an estimated one-third of which are suicides.

34. Minorities account for a disproportionate percentage of the daily jail population.

35. Minimum security prisons operate without armed guards or walls.

36. Evaluation of specific halfway house programs has indicated strong support for the success of this type of treatment.

37. The first penal institutions were often operated under a "fee system" whereby inmates were required to pay for their own food and services.

38. The Federal correctional policy is bifurcated, with the goals of keeping as many nonviolent offenders out of the system and incarcerating dangerous offenders for longer periods of time.

39. Less than one quarter of the jailed inmates are unconvicted.

40. The personal profile of a typical jail inmate differs significantly from the profile of an average arrestee.

41. There are more women than men in jail on drug-related offenses.

42. Currently, prison systems in four states are under court orders related to overcrowding.

43. In New York, overcrowding has prompted the city to employ river barges as "floating jails" anchored offshore.

MULTIPLE CHOICE

44.   Wergild is a historical term with which of the following meanings.

       a.   incarceration
       b.   rehabilitation
       c.   institution
       d.   restitution

45.   In 1787, the "Philadelphia Society for Alleviating the Miseries of Public Prisons" was
       formed by which group.

       a.   Mormons
       b.   Quakers
       c.   Mennonites
       d.   Moonies

46.   Which of the following was the philosophy of crime prevention in the Auburn system.

       a.   fear of punishment
       b.   silence/isolation
       c.   physical torture
       d.   both a and b

47.   The Auburn Prison design became known as the _____ system.

       a.   tier
       b.   hierarchical
       c.   semicircular
       d.   none of the above

48.   Today's American prisons, are most similar to which of the following.

       a.   Auburn system
       b.   Eastern system
       c.   Walnut system
       d.   Pennsylvania system

49.   When prison officials sold the labor of inmates to private business; this was known as which of the following.

      a.   state account system
      b.   convict-lease system
      c.   contract system
      d.   none of the above

50.   The first reformatory programs in the United States were initiated by which of the following people.

      a.   William Penn
      b.   Thomas Mott Osborne
      c.   Z.R. Brockway
      d.   Steve Smith

51.   The nation's jails are institutional facilities serving which purpose.

      a.   hold convicted offenders awaiting sentence
      b.   detain accused offenders who cannot make bail
      c.   house felons when state prisons are overcrowded
      d.   all of the above

52.   According to recent statistics, approximately _____ percent of inmates in the nation's jails are unconvicted.

      a.   10%
      b.   25%
      c.   50%
      d.   60%

53.   The average daily jail population is approximately _____ jail inmates.

      a.   350,000
      b.   468,000
      c.   570,000
      d.   820,000

54.   Typically, jails are under the jurisdiction of _____ government.

      a.   city
      b.   county
      c.   state
      d.   federal

55. Jails are usually administered under which concept.

    a. custodial convenience
    b. correctional service
    c. preventive detention
    d. security maintenance

56. The annual jail inmate turnover rate is about _____ million.

    a. 5
    b. 10
    c. 15
    d. 20

57. Which of the following are the most common occupants of minimum security prisons.

    a. misdemeanants
    b. white-collar criminals
    c. blue collar criminals
    d. auto thieves

58. Which of the following conditions helps to explain the significant rise in correctional populations.

    a. offenders not making bail
    b. increased incarceration sentencing laws
    c. high unemployment rates
    d. all of the above

MATCHING

59. Halfway House   A.   Congregate System

60. Prison   B.   Single Cell Habitation

61. Walnut Street Jail   C.   Community Corrections

62. Auburn Prison   D.   Quakers

63. Pennsylvania System   E.   Incapacitation

64. Punishment Reform   F.   Solitary Cells

ESSAY QUESTIONS

65.   Describe the Auburn system; what characteristics of this system remain in our prisons today?

66.   Explain the philosophy of "custodial convenience."

67.   What is the difference between maximum, medium, and minimum security prisons?

68.   Describe several problems with jail conditions and several ways jail crowding may be alleviated.

69.   Discuss several approaches to community corrections and whether or not such approaches should be used to reduce prison overcrowding.

70.   Do you agree or disagree with private participation in corrections? Why or why not?

CHAPTER FIFTEEN ANSWER SECTION

FILL-IN REVIEW

1. corrections, treatment, punishment
2. recidivism, half
3. John Howard's
4. William Penn
5. solitary, isolation
6. penitentiary
7. Auburn, punishment
8. single
9. semicircle, circumference
10. convict-lease
11. humanitarianism
12. Sumners-Ashurst
13. prisoner rights
14. county, conditions
15. custodial convenience, standards
16. overcrowding
17. maximum, medium, minimum
18. maxi-maxi
19. shock incarceration
20. reintegrate
21. halfway, release
22. private

SELF TEST

True/False

23.	T		34.	T
24.	F		35.	T
25.	F		36.	F
26.	F		37.	T
27.	F		38.	T
28.	T		39.	F
29.	T		40.	F
30.	F		41.	T
31.	T		42.	F
32.	F		43.	T
33.	T			

MULTIPLE CHOICE

44.	D	52.	C
45.	B	53.	C
46.	D	54.	B
47.	A	55.	A
48.	A	56.	D
49.	C	57.	B
50.	C	58.	D
51.	D		

MATCHING

59.	C
60.	G
61.	F
62.	A
63.	B
64.	D

16   The Prison Experience: Living in and Leaving Prison

LEARNING OBJECTIVES

1.   Explain the meaning of total institutions and the prisonization process.

2.   List several characteristics of both male and female prison inmates, and the difference in cultures between female and male institutions.

3.   Differentiate among the thief, convict, and conventional subcultures.

4.   Describe the impact of racial tensions on the inmate subculture.

5.   Explain the concepts of vocational training, prison industry, education, and self-help groups, and describe their role in the prison system.

6.   List several potential advantages and disadvantages of conjugal visits.

7.   Describe the personal characteristics and the role of the typical prison guard.

8.   Describe the extent of prison violence and list possible causes for such violence.

9.   Describe the three models of prison management.

10.   Define the hands-off doctrine.

11.   Describe the significance of the Federal Civil Rights Act regarding prisoners' complaints and detail the evolution of major substantive rights for prison inmates.

12.   Define the exceptional circumstances doctrine.

13.   Describe the criteria used by the Courts in determining whether a punishment constitutes cruel and unusual conduct.

14.   Define parole.

15.   List the four primary functions of parole board.

16.   Explain why many released inmates have a difficult time adjusting to general society.

CHAPTER SUMMARY

The portrait of the average inmate includes several common characteristics: young, male, minority, poor, drug/alcohol abuser, undereducated, recidivist, and violent. The most common offenses among the prison population were robbery, drug trafficking and burglary. Women are generally arrested for about 20% of index crimes and 11% of all violent crimes, yet female inmates account for only 6% of the prison population. While the typical male inmate was a violent offender, female inmates tended to commit drug offenses.

Erving Goffman has suggested that American prisons are **total institutions**, with inmates completely segregated from the outside world. Keith Farrington has countered that theory claiming prisons are **not-so-total institutions**, as they can never be completely insulated from society, considering the constant flow of goods and the freedom of staff in the external world.

Inmates must learn to adjust to prison life. Some turn to the black market, or the hustle, selling illegal commodities. Many, finding themselves confronted by racial conflict, resort to segregation. Some seek to find their niche in the institution. Most have a tendency to adhere to the unwritten rules of the **inmate subculture**.

The female crime rate is rising at a rate much faster than the male rate. Combined with mandatory and determinate sentencing, the result has been an increased number of female prisoners. Women's institutions tend to be less secure and smaller than mens. Female inmates, like their male counterparts, have a tendency to be young, single, minority and undereducated. One problem associated especially with female incarceration is the disruption of family life.

Almost every prison facility employs some mode of treatment for inmates. This may come in the form of group **counseling, educational,** or **vocational** training. To supplement programs stressing rehabilitation, a number of states have implemented **work-release** or furlough programs, where the deserving inmates leave the institution and hold regular jobs in the community. **Conjugal visits** are another form of treatment where prisoners are able to have private meetings with their wives and family on a regular basis. Finally, prisoners are normally expected to work within the institution as part of their treatment program in areas such as food services, maintenance, laundry, and agriculture. Problems with such programs include inadequate funding and administration as well as the growing number of special-needs inmates such as mentally ill, elderly, drug-dependent, and AIDS-infected prisoners.

There are approximately 120,000 correctional officers staffing penal institutions. Such officers generally receive little pre-service training. Lucien Lombardo has described correctional officers as "people workers," with no particular animosity to inmates. The correctional officer faces a dual role of advocating treatment and rehabilitation while maintaining security and order.

The Prison Experience: Living in and Leaving Prison

One concern for prison administrators is prison violence including personal attacks and thefts. Some theorists believe inmates are prone to violence while others suggest prison conditions, such as overcrowding, and prison mismanagement, such as ineffective grievance procedures, contribute to violent behavior. Some have suggested reforming prison management in hopes of alleviating this problem.

Prior to 1960, it was accepted that upon conviction an incarcerated individual forfeited all rights not expressly granted by statutory law or correctional policy. State and federal courts were reluctant to intervene in the administration of prisons unless the circumstances of a case clearly indicated a serious breach of the Eighth Amendment's protection against cruel and unusual punishment; this judicial policy is referred to as the **hands-off doctrine**. As the 1960's drew to a close, however, the hands-off doctrine underwent a process of erosion when activist groups began to utilize. In the 1964 case of **Cooper v. Pate**, the Supreme Court recognized the right of prisoners to sue for civil rights violations in cases involving religious freedom. While this case applied to a narrow issue, it opened the door to providing other rights for inmates.

A major concern for the prisoners' rights movement was to increase the substantive rights of inmates. These rights include: access to courts, legal services and materials; freedom of the press and expression; freedom of religion; medical rights; freedom from cruel and unusual punishment; and the right to minimum conditions necessary for survival. Since 1980, a more conservative Court has curtailed some rights of prisoners, reverting to the hands-off doctrine.

Parole is the planned community release and supervision of incarcerated offenders prior to the actual expiration of their prison sentences. It is usually considered a way of completing a prison sentence in the community. The decision to parole is determined by statutory requirement and usually involves completion of a minimum sentence, less any good-time or special release credits.

Parole is usually granted by the **parole board,** whose task is to review inmate cases and determine whether an offender has reached a rehabilitative level sufficient to deal with the outside world. The actual parole decision is made at a **parole grant hearing**. At this time the full board or a selected subcommittee reviews information, may meet with the offender, and then decides whether the parole applicant has a reasonable probability of succeeding outside of prison. Before being released into the community, a parolee is supplied with a set of **parole rules** that guide their behavior and sets limits on their activities. If, at any time, these rules are violated, the offender can be returned to the institution to serve the remainder of the sentence; this is known as a **technical parole violation**. The offender's parole can also be **revoked** by committing a new offense while in the community.

Chapter 16

KEY TERMS AND CONCEPTS

Total Institutions
Hustle
Niche
Mature Coping
Inmate Subculture
Argot
Prisonization
Right Guy
Importation Model
Thief Subculture
Convict Subculture
Conventional Subculture
Make-Believe Family
Self-Mutilation
Counseling
Special-Needs Inmate
AIDS
Vocational Training
Work-Release
Free Venture Program
Conjugal Visit
Hudson v. Palmer
Jackson v. Bishop
Parole
Procedural Rights
Technical Parole Violation
Parole Board

Dothard v. Rawlinson
Prison Violence
Overcrowding
Self-Governance
Consensual Model
Responsibility Model
Control Model
Hands-Off Doctrine
Federal Civil Rights Act
Cooper v. Pate
Turner v. Safley
Procunier v. Martinez
Numin v. Phelps
Exceptional Circumstances Doctrine
Newman v. Alabama
Estelle v. Gamble
Cruel and Unusual Punishment
Rhodes v. Chapman
Estelle v. Ruiz
Johnson v. Avery
Farmer v. Brennan
Parole Rules
Salient Factor Score
Intense Supervision Probation (ISP)
Parole Revocation
Civil Death

FILL-IN REVIEW

1. _____ provides inmates with a source of steady income and the satisfaction that they are beating the _____.

2. An inmate's _____ is a kind of insulation from the pains of imprisonment.

3. Passed on from one generation of inmates to another, the inmate _____ _____ represents the values of interpersonal relations within the prison.

4. Prisoners have a unique language or _____ which they use.

The Prison Experience: Living in and Leaving Prison

5.   An inmate's assimilation into the existing prison culture is known as the
        _____ process.

6.   The term for an inmate who conforms to the rules of the inmate culture is the
        "_____ _____."

7.   The _____ _____ model suggests that the inmate _____ is
        affected as much by values of newcomers as it is by traditional inmate values.

8.   Irwin and Cressey found that the inmate world was divided into three groups, each
        corresponding to a role in the outside world: the _____ subculture, the
        _____ subculture, and the _____ subculture.

9.   A form of adaptation to prison used by women is the _____-_____
        family, a quasi-kinship group which provides warm, stable relationships.

10.   In addition to individual analysis and group processes, inmate rehabilitation may also be
        pursued through _____ or _____ training.

11.   _____-_____programs allow deserving inmates to leave the
        institution and hold regular jobs in the _____, often returning to the facility
        at night.

12.   During _____ visits prisoners are able to have completely
        _____ meetings with spouses and family on a regular basis.

13.   The typical _____ prison is a small, low security institution, predominantly
        of one gender and populated by _____, carefully screened offenders.

14.   Most prominent among prison _____ are those designed to help maintain
        and run the _____ and provide services for other public or state facilities.

15.   The greatest problem faced by prison guards is the duality of their role: maintainer of
        _____ and _____; advocate of _____
        and _____.

16.   When inmates break prison rules, they are subject to _____ action
        measured within the institution.

17.   A recent trend in prisons which may be associated with violence is the
        _____ caused by rapid increases in the prison _____.

18.   Prior to 1960, it was accepted that upon _____ an individual forfeited all
        _____not expressly granted by statutory law or correctional policy.

Chapter 16

19. The _____-_____ doctrine is a judicial policy whereby state and federal _____ are reluctant to intervene in the operations of prisons.

20. The _____ _____ _____ Act serves as the fundamental basis on which courts have opened their doors to prisoner rights cases.

21. In the 1964 case of *Cooper v. Pate*, the U.S. Supreme Court ruled that inmates who were being denied the right to practice their _____ were entitled to legal redress.

22. The Supreme Court decision in the _____ case, substantially restricted prison officials in their _____ of prisoners' mail.

23. The courts maintained their distance in medical rights cases through the _____ _____ doctrine.

24. In the *Newman* case, the entire _____ prison system's _____ facilities were declared inadequate.

25. In *Estelle v. Gamble*, the U.S. Supreme Court clearly stated the inmate's right to _____care.

26. Parole is the planned community _____ and supervision of incarcerated offenders prior to actual expiration of their _____ sentences.

27. If a _____ violates the rules, he or she can be returned to the institution to serve the remainder of the sentence; this is known as a _____ parole violation.

28. Parole _____ may curtail or prohibit certain types of _____ while encouraging or demanding others.

SELF TEST

True/False

29. A common practice among female inmates is "carving," or mutilation of their bodies.

30. One problem associated with conjugal visitation is the lack of appropriate facilities.

31. Scientific evaluation of work release programs indicates that they tend to be effective in reducing recidivism rates.

32. A national study showed that correctional rehabilitative efforts have a significant effect on recidivism.

33.   Prisons holding more than 1,000 inmates are still common in the United States.

34.   Many heterosexual men will turn to homosexual relationships when faced with long prison sentences.

35.   It is quite likely that there is a correlation between prison overcrowding and violence.

36.   The device most widely used to bring prisoners' complaints before state and federal courts was the Federal Civil Liberties Act.

37.   Today, the courts maintain their distance in medical rights cases through the exceptional circumstances doctrine.

38.   Cruel and unusual punishment has never been specifically defined by the U.S. Supreme Court.

39.   Courts have ruled that solitary confinement and corporal punishment are cruel and unusual.

40.   In *Hudson v. Palmer*, the U.S. Supreme Court ruled that inmates have a Fourth Amendment right to privacy over materials contained in their cells.

41.   Research has indicated that discipline has suffered because of the inclusion of women into the prison guard force.

42.   The most common offenses for prison inmates were robbery, drug trafficking and burglary.

43.   Prison rule violations are associated with young inmates with low IQs and many juvenile convictions.

44.   The Black Power movement created racial tensions and significantly altered the inmate subculture.

45.   Less than one in twenty female inmates is pregnant at intake or has given birth within the previous year.

46.   Counseling is the most common prison treatment strategy.

47.   According to the U.S. Supreme Court's decision in *Dothard v. Rawlinson*, it is acceptable for a facility to refuse to hire a female correctional officer based on potential danger from male inmates.

48.   If special religious needs of inmates will cause other groups to make similar demands or they are cumbersome or impossible to implement due to cost or security, they can be denied.

49.   Parole is the planned community release and supervision of offenders before any of their prison sentence has been served.

50.   "Civil death statutes" have generally been ruled constitutional.

51.   Over a quarter of the states allow for the termination of parental rights for felony convictions, and/or imprisonment.

52.   The social, psychological, and economic conditions which may have led a person to crime, generally remain unchanged upon release from prison.

MULTIPLE CHOICE

53.   Recent figures suggest that the number of releases paroled has _____, and number of mandatory releases has _____ .

    a.   decreased, increased
    b.   increased, decreased
    c.   increased, increased
    d.   decreased, decreased

54.   Irwin and Cressey found that prisoners among the _____ subculture always try to "do their own time."

    a.   convict
    b.   thief
    c.   conventional
    d.   none of the above

55.   The actual parole decision is made at a parole _____ _____ .

    a.   board hearing
    b.   review committee
    c.   board review
    d.   grant hearing

56.   National estimates are that approximately _____ in every 100,000 inmates are HIV positive; twenty times the national average.

    a.   50
    b.   150
    c.   360
    d.   500

The Prison Experience: Living in and Leaving Prison

57. There are approximately _____ correctional officers working in the nations state prison facilities.

    a. 50,000
    b. 120,000
    c. 330,000
    d. 400,000

58. An analysis of prison guards suggests that they have which of the following attitudes.

    a. no particular animosity toward inmates
    b. favor a punishment orientation for inmates
    c. favor rehabilitation efforts for inmates
    d. both a and c

59. Violations of prison rules may result in disciplinary action against the inmate, which may affect which of the following.

    a. good time
    b. transfer
    c. privileges
    d. all of the above

60. Most prison experts agree that a minimum of _____ square feet is needed for each prison inmate.

    a. 30
    b. 50
    c. 60
    d. 90

61. Which of the following may cause prison violence.

    a. inhumane conditions
    b. violence-prone inmates
    c. prison mismanagement
    d. all of the above

62. What is the basis for prisoner right cases in the courts.

    a. Federal Civil Rights Act
    b. procedural rights
    c. Eighth Amendment
    d. hands-off doctrine

Chapter 16

63.   In what area did the courts first lift the hands-off doctrine.

     a.   freedom of the press
     b.   freedom of religion
     c.   freedom to medical treatment
     d.   freedom from cruel and unusual punishment

64.   Which of the following cases dealt with the censorship of an inmate's mail.

     a.   *Sostre v. McGinnis*
     b.   *Wolff v. McDonel*
     c.   *Procunier v. Martinez*
     d.   *Sostre v. Rockefeller*

65.   Under the hands-off doctrine, unless the circumstances of a case clearly indicated a serious breach of _____ rights, the courts would avoid dealing with correctional administrative matters.

     a.   First Amendment
     b.   Fifth Amendment
     c.   Eighth Amendment
     d.   Fourteenth Amendment

66.   Which U.S. Supreme Court case established a right to medical care for inmates.

     a.   *Cooper v. Pate*
     b.   *Estelle v. Gamble*
     c.   *Newman v. Alabama*
     d.   *Bell v. Wolfish*

67.   For what right did the courts use the "exceptional circumstances" doctrine.

     a.   right to medical treatment
     b.   freedom from cruel and unusual punishment
     c.   right to privacy
     d.   freedom of religion

68.   The concept of cruel and unusual punishment is founded in the _____ Amendment of the U.S. Constitution.

     a.   First
     b.   Fifth
     c.   Eighth
     d.   Fourteenth

69.   What percentage of inmates are released from prison after serving their entire sentence, without any good-time forgiven.

    a.   1%
    b.   5%
    c.   10%
    d.   15%

70.   Approximately how many inmates escape from federal and state prisons every year.

    a.   3,000
    b.   7,000
    c.   12,000
    d.   16,000

71.   What percentage of parole-release decisions are made by a parole board.

    a.   40
    b.   50
    c.   60
    d.   70

72.   What percentage of female prisoners claim to have been physically and/or sexually abused.

    a.   20%
    b.   40%
    c.   60%
    d.   80%

73.   Which model of prison management stresses clearly defined rules of behavior and top-down leadership.

    a.   consensual model
    b.   responsibility model
    c.   conformity model
    d.   control model

MATCHING

74.	*Hudson v. Palmer*	A.	Medical facilities declared inadequate
75.	*Estelle v. Gamble*	B.	Inmate's right to privacy
76.	*Rhodes v. Chapman*	C.	Established inmate's right to medical care
77.	*Procunier v. Martinez*	D.	Allowed more than one inmate in a single cell
78.	*Newman v. Alabama*	E.	Dealt with the censorship of prisoner correspondence
79.	*Jackson v. Bishop*	F.	Ended corporal punishment
80.	Parole Rules	G.	Prohibit certain behavior

ESSAY QUESTIONS

81. Give several reasons why prison industries should or should not be given high priority.

82. Should inmates be allowed to have conjugal visits? Why or why not?

83. Discuss several explanations regarding the causes of prison violence. What, if anything can be done to alleviate such violence?

84. Should female correctional officers be allowed to work in male institutions? Why or why not?

85. Discuss three basic justifications for the courts' neglect of prison conditions; have justifications changed in the 1990's?

86. Describe the exceptional circumstances doctrine and the significance attached to this doctrine.

87. What constitutes cruel and unusual punishment? Explain what types of prison issues have typically been concerned with this question.

The Prison Experience: Living in and Leaving Prison

88. What are the primary functions of a parole board?

89. In your opinion, what qualification would be important for members of a parole board?

90. What are the primary considerations taken into account by a parole board in determining release.

91. Should parole boards have greater or less discretion? Explain.

92. Identify the procedures in parole revocation. What are the rights of the parolee?

CHAPTER SIXTEEN ANSWER SECTION

FILL-IN REVIEW

1. Hustling, system
2. niche
3. social code
4. argot
5. prisonization
6. right guy
7. importation, culture
8. thief, convict, conventional
9. make-believe
10. vocational, educational
11. Work-release, community
12. conjugal, private
13. coed, nonviolent
14. industries, institution
15. order, security, treatment, rehabilitation
16. discipline
17. overcrowding, population
18. conviction, rights
19. hands-off, courts
20. Federal Civil Rights
21. religion
22. *Procunier*, censorship
23. exceptional circumstances
24. Alabama, medical
25. medical
26. release, prison
27. parolee, technical
28. rules, behavior

SELF TEST

True/False

29.	T	41.	F
30.	T	42.	T
31.	F	43.	T
32.	F	44.	T
33.	T	45.	F
34.	T	46.	T
35.	T	47.	T
36.	F	48.	T
37.	F	49.	F
38.	T	50.	F
39.	F	51.	T
40.	F	52.	T

MULTIPLE CHOICE

53.	D	64.	C
54.	C	65.	C
55.	B	66.	B
56.	B	67.	D
57.	A	68.	B
58.	C	69.	D
59.	B	70.	B
60.	D	71.	A
61.	D	72.	C
62.	C	73.	C
63.	D	74.	B

MATCHING

74.	B
75.	C
76.	D
77.	E
78.	A
79.	F
80.	G

17   Juvenile Justice

LEARNING OBJECTIVES

1. Contrast the due process and *parens patriae* approaches to the juvenile justice system.

2. Describe the Poor Laws and the Chancery Court.

3. Explain the paternalistic nature of the juvenile court in its early form.

4. Explain the significance of the following three U.S. Supreme Court decisions: *Kent v. United States*, *In re Gault*, and *In re Winship*.

5. Describe the intake process.

6. Differentiate between delinquents and status offenders.

7. Compare and contrast the juvenile and adult justice systems.

8. Explain the controversies regarding waiving a juvenile to adult court.

9. Explain the problems associated with detaining juveniles in adult jails.

10. Describe the juvenile trial process.

11. Using U.S. Supreme Court case law, describe the juvenile's right to receive treatment if committed to a juvenile institution.

CHAPTER SUMMARY

The **juvenile justice system** deals with two categories of juvenile offenders: **delinquents** and **status offenders**. Early juvenile courts were based on the philosophy of *parens patriae*; that is, the idea that the state was to act on behalf of the parent in the interest of the child. The first comprehensive juvenile court was established in Illinois in 1899. In its early form, the juvenile court was considered paternalistic and provided youth with quasi-legal, personalized justice. In the 1960's and 1970's, the Supreme Court radically altered the juvenile justice system by ruling on a series of cases which established due process rights for juveniles. Supreme Court cases such as *Kent v. United States*, *In re Gault*, and *In re Winship* made the juvenile justice process more similar to its adult counterpart. Today, the juvenile court seeks to promote the **rehabilitation** of the child within a framework of procedural **due process**.

During the investigatory and arrest stages of the juvenile process, the police generally have more discretion than they do when dealing with adult offenders. Once taken into custody, however, the juvenile is protected by most of the procedural safeguards awarded to adults -- including the right to counsel and the privilege against self-incrimination. Juveniles have not, however, been granted a constitutional right to a jury trial.

After arrest and before trial, the juvenile defendant is processed through a number of stages which may include **intake**, **detention**, **bail**, **waiver hearing** and **diversion** programs. As a further distinction from the adult justice system, the Supreme Court, in the case of *Schall v. Martin*, upheld the right of the states to detain a child before trial in order to protect their welfare and the public safety. There are, however, serious issues in juvenile detention including the problems related to youths detained in adult jails. Another important issue in the juvenile justice system is the waiver process which transfers juvenile offenders to adult criminal courts. A federally sponsored survey identified several serious problems related to youths processed in adult courts.

Juvenile court judges have broad discretionary power in the sentencing of juveniles with dispositions ranging from dismissal to probation to institutional commitment. Recent trends in sentencing include the "get tough" approach with dangerous offenders, the removal of status and minor offenders from the system, and a shift in philosophy to the concept of "just deserts." Despite these trends, most jurisdictions continue to focus on rehabilitation as a primary dispositional goal. This is evident in recent Supreme Court decisions which have indicated that youth who are committed to a juvenile institution have a "right" to receive treatment.

Chapter 17

KEY TERMS AND CONCEPTS

Juvenile Justice System
Parens Patriae
Poor Laws
Apprenticeship
Chancery Courts
Child-Saving Movement
Child Savers
House of Refuge
Children's Aid Society
Illinois Juvenile Court Act
McKeiver v. Pennsylvania
New Jersey v. T.L.O.
Intake
Detention
Schall v. Martin
Bail
Plea Bargaining
Waiver of Jurisdiction
Disposition
Juvenile Justice and Delinquency
Prevention Act of 1974 (JJDP Act)
Office of Juvenile Justice and
Delinquency Prevention (OJJ DP)

Cottage System
Kent v. United States
In re Gault
In re Winship
Breed v. Jones
Due Process
Status Offender
Transfer
Waiver
School Searches
Vernonia School District v. Acton
Treatment
Sentencing
"Get Tough" Approach
Probation
Balanced Probation
Institutionalization
Wilkins v. Missouri
Postdisposition
Inmates v. Affleck
Nelson v. Heyne
Morales v. Turman
Deinstitutionalization of Status
Offenders (DSO)

FILL-IN REVIEW

1.   The philosophy of _____ _____ refers to the state
        acting in the interest of the child on behalf of the parent.

2.   _____ Laws allowed for the appointment of overseers indenture poor or
        neglected children as _____.

3.   _____ was a practice where children were placed in the care of adults who
        taught them a trade.

4.   During the middle ages, _____ _____ were concerned
        primarily with protecting property rights, although its authority extended to the welfare of
        children in general.

198

Juvenile Justice

5.   One of the most concrete examples of institutional care for juveniles in early America was the _____ of _____.

6.   The first comprehensive juvenile court was developed in _____ in 1899.

7.   _____ _____ include truants and habitually disobedient and ungovernable children.

8.   Today's juvenile court system embodies both _____ and _____ orientations.

9.   Juvenile court _____ is established by state statute and is based on several factors, the first of which is _____.

10.   The _____ stage represents an opportunity to place a child in informal programs both within the court and in the _____.

11.   After a juvenile is taken into custody, a decision is usually made whether to release the child to the parent or guardian or _____ the child in a Shelter pending _____.

12.   In the case of _____ v. _____ the U.Supreme Court upheld the right of the States to detain a child before trial in order to protect their welfare and public _____.

13.   Today most jurisdictions provide by statute for_____, or transfer, of juvenile offenders to the _____ courts.

14.   The U.S. Supreme Court in _____ v. _____ held that the waiver proceeding was a critically important stage in the juvenile process and that juveniles must be afforded _____ requirements of due process of law at such proceedings.

15.   There has been a trend toward giving _____ jurisdiction for juvenile crimes to the adult courts and then allowing _____ the power to waive deserving cases back to the juvenile authorities.

16.   In the landmark case of_____, the U.S. Supreme Court ruled that the concept of fundamental _____ be made applicable to juvenile delinquency proceedings.

17.   The *In re Gault* decision gave juveniles similar procedural safeguards as adults at trial proceedings, including the right to_____, the right to confront _____, and the privilege against_____ - _____, and has indirectly influenced and reinforced juvenile *Miranda* rights.

18.   In the _____ case, the U.S. Supreme Court ruled that the standard in a criminal prosecution of "_____ beyond a _____ _____ " is also required in the adjudication of a delinquency petition.

19.   Graduated sanctions provide a range of options, moving from the least to the most _____ placement for different offenders.

20.   Standards for the juvenile justice system set forth by the American Bar Association suggest a shift in juvenile court philosophy, from traditional _____ to the concept of "_____ _____."

21.   The most severe of the statutory disposition available to the juvenile court involves committing the child to a juvenile _____.

22.   A priority of recent years has been the effort to treat the hard core, _____ delinquent while removing non-violent and non-criminal youth from the juvenile _____ system.

23.   The _____ v. _____ case is significant because it was the first federal court of appeals decision to affirm a constitutional right of juveniles to _____.

24.   The _____ - _____ movement was based on the belief that urban and immigrant youths were prone to criminal deviance and immorality and might be _____ by state intervention.

SELF TEST

True/False

25.   The philosophy *parens patriae* is that the state is to act on behalf of the parent in the interests of the child.

26.   Attorney representation has always been required for juveniles.

27.   Status offenders are youths who engage in acts that are considered in violation of the penal code.

28.   School officials may search students without probable cause or at any time in order to determine whether they are in possession of contraband such as drugs or weapons.

29.   The practice of detaining juveniles in adult jails still continues today.

30. The majority of states have passed laws that give adult courts original jurisdiction for many offenses committed by juveniles.

31. Delinquents and status offenders are frequently held in joint custody.

32. The right to receive *Miranda* warnings is applicable to juveniles as well as to adults.

33. The main concern of the juvenile court, in its early form, was adherence to legal doctrine versus the "best interest of the child."

34. Unlike adults, where sole criteria for pretrial release is availability for trial, juveniles may be detained for other reasons, including his or her own protection.

35. Juvenile courts deal only with conduct of delinquent behavior.

36. The term "intake" refers to the informal processing of cases by the juvenile court.

37. Plea bargaining is a fairly common practice in the juvenile justice system.

38. The two major criteria for waiver are the age of the child and the type of offense alleged in the petition.

39. In the case of *In re Winship*, the U.S. Supreme Court found that only a "preponderance of the evidence" is required in the adjudication of a delinquency petition.

40. Minority youths comprise more than half of the juveniles in public facilities.

41. If conditions of parole are violated, the juvenile may have parole revoked and be returned to the institution.

42. The Juvenile Justice and Delinquency Prevention Act of 1974 (JJDP Act) established the federal office of Juvenile Justice and Delinquency Prevention (OJJDP).

43. The number of juvenile delinquency cases decreased from 1985 through 1994.

44. The purpose of aftercare is to help youths to make the transition from institutional life.

Chapter 17

MULTIPLE CHOICE

45.   The first separate juvenile court system was established in:

    a.   New York
    b.   California
    c.   Illinois
    d.   Massachusetts

46.   The early juvenile court movement was which of the following.

    a.   adversarial
    b.   paternalistic
    c.   punitive
    d.   none of the above

47.   About _____ youths under 18 years of age are arrested each year.

    a.   one million
    b.   one and a half million
    c.   Two million
    d.   two and a half million

48.   The U.S. Supreme Court case of _____ v. _____ held that the school's right to maintain discipline on school grounds allowed them to search a student and their possessions as a safety precaution.

    a.   *Kent v. United States*
    b.   *Schall v. Martin*
    c.   *Fare v. Michael C.*
    d.   *New Jersey v. T.L.O.*

49.   The majority of the state and federal courts hold that a juvenile does <u>not</u> have the right to which of the following.

    a.   due process
    b.   bail
    c.   counsel
    d.   confront witnesses

50. A federal sponsored study found that children confined in adult institutions were
    _____ times as likely to commit suicide as those placed in detention
    center exclusively for juveniles.

    a.   two
    b.   five
    c.   eight
    d.   twenty

51. Which of the following cases dealt with the waiver process for juveniles.

    a.   *People v. Overton*
    b.   *Kent v. United States*
    c.   *In re Winship*
    d.   none of the above

52. When a juvenile is transferred to a criminal court, it is called:

    a.   waiver
    b.   diversion
    c.   disposition
    d.   parens patriae

53. Juveniles are allowed to be tried as adults in criminal courts in which way(s).

    a.   concurrent jurisdiction
    b.   excluded offenses
    c.   judicial waiver
    d.   all of the above

54. Which disposition is most commonly used in juvenile court.

    a.   dismissal
    b.   probation
    c.   suspended judgment
    d.   diversion

55. Which of the following cases in juvenile proceedings established due process standards at the
    pretrial, trial and post-trial stages.

    a.   *Ken v. United States*
    b.   *In re Gault*
    c.   *In re Winship*
    d.   *Morales v. Turman*

Chapter 17

56. In which case did the Supreme Court hold that the standard of proof beyond a reasonable doubt is required at the adjudication of a delinquency petition.

    a. *In re Winship*
    b. *Kent v. United States*
    c. *Schall v. Martin*
    d. none of the above

57. Which of the following cases held that trial by jury in juvenile court's adjudicative stage is not a constitutional requirement.

    a. *Kent v. United States*
    b. *In re Winship*
    c. *In re Gault*
    d. *McKeiver v. Pennsylvania*

58. During the 1960s, the one **exception** of rights given to juveniles was which of the following.

    a. right to counsel
    b. right to jury trial
    c. right to cross-examine witnesses
    d. right to protection against double jeopardy

59. Which of the following case(s) held that institutionalized juveniles have a statutory right to treatment

    a. *Inmates v. Affleck*
    b. *Nelson v. Heyne*
    c. *Morales v. Turman*
    d. all of the above

60. Which of the following case(s) dealt with the age requirement for the application of the death penalty.

    a. *Wilkins v. Missouri*
    b. *Stanford v. Kentucky*
    c. both a and b
    d. neither a nor b

MATCHING

61.	*In re Winship*	A.	Waiver process
62.	*In re Gault*	B.	Beyond a reasonable doubt standard
63.	*Inmates v. Affleck*	C.	School searches
64.	*New Jersey v. T.L.O.*	D.	No right of jury trial
65.	*Schall v. Martin*	E.	Fundamental fairness
66.	*Kent v. United States*	F.	Denial of pretrial release
67.	*McKeiver v. Pennsylvania*	G.	Right to treatment

ESSAY QUESTIONS

68. Discuss the nature and significance of "status" offenses.

69. What factors establish court jurisdiction over a juvenile?

70. What is waiver of jurisdiction? Under what conditions should juveniles be processed in adult courts?

71. Discuss the significance of the *In re Gault* and *In re Winship* cases.

72. Discuss whether or not you agree with the principle of a death penalty for minors.

73. Should juveniles be given mandatory incarceration sentences for serious crimes as adults are? Explain.

74. Describe some of the major programs effecting juvenile justice today.

CHAPTER SEVENTEEN ANSWER SECTION

FILL-IN REVIEW

1. *parens patriae*
2. Poor, servants
3. Apprenticeship
4. Chancery Courts
5. House, Refuge
6. Illinois
7. Status offenders
8. rehabilitative, legalistic
9. jurisdiction, age
10. intake, community
11. detain, trial
12. *Schall v. Martin*, safety
13. waiver, criminal
14. *Kent v. United States*, minimum
15. original, judges
16. *In re Gault*, fairness
17. counsel, witnesses, self-incrimination
18. *In re Winship*, proof, reasonable doubt
19. restrictive
20. rehabilitation, just deserts
21. institution
22. chronic, correctional
23. *Nelson v. Heyne*, treatment
24. child-saving, saved

SELF TEST

True/False

25.	T	35.	F
26.	F	36.	F
27.	F	37.	F
28.	T	38.	T
29.	T	39.	F
30.	T	40.	T
31.	T	41.	T
32.	T	42.	T
33.	F	43.	F
34.	T	44.	T

MULTIPLE CHOICE

45.	C	53.	D
46.	B	54.	B
47.	C	55.	B
48.	D	56.	A
49.	B	57.	D
50.	C	58.	B
51.	B	59.	D
52.	A	60.	C

MATCHING

61.	B
62.	E
63.	G
64.	C
65.	F
66.	A
67.	D